Second Helpings

Second Helpings

Books and Activities About Food

Jan Irving
Robin Currie

Illustrated by Susie Kropa

Peddler's Pack Series No. 3

1994
TEACHER IDEAS PRESS
A Division of
Libraries Unlimited, Inc.
Englewood, Colorado

TEACHER IDEAS PRESS
A Division of Libraries Unlimited, Inc.
P.O. Box 6633
Englewood, CO 80155-6633
1-800-237-6124

Project Editor: Kevin W. Perizzolo
Copy Editor: Jason Cook
Proofreader: Eileen Bartlett
Typesetting and Interior Design: Judy Gay Matthews

Library of Congress Cataloging-in-Publication Data

Irving, Jan, 1942–
    Second helpings : books and activities about food / Jan Irving, Robin Currie.
    xii, 145 p. 22x28 cm. -- (Peddler's pack series ; no. 3)
    Includes bibliographical references and index.
    ISBN 1-56308-073-7 (softbound)
    1. Food--Study and teaching (Primary) 2. Libraries, Children's--Activity programs. 3. Activity programs in education. I. Currie, Robin, 1948–   . II. Title. III. Series.
    TX364.I787 1994
    372.3'7--dc20   94-7370
                                                              CIP

*We offer special thanksgiving
to Barbara and Jeff,
who have nurtured our spirits.*

Contents

Introduction

Second Helpings is our second source book for teachers, librarians, and caregivers on the topic of food. It is a sequel of sorts to *Mudluscious*, but with significant differences. The activities are planned for older children, primary through middle elementary grades. The sections of each chapter have changed. The Related Activities are more curricular than simply a collection of stories, songs, poems, crafts, and games. Stories, scripts, and some of the shorter related activities are still included, but often as springboards for children to create their own. There is a stronger emphasis on language activities, curricular connections, and multicultural titles.

Books about baked goods and silly foods are still published in large quantities. Soup, gardening, shopping for food, preparing food, and lunch all remain topics popular enough for new titles. With the demand for more multicultural titles, a dramatic increase in the amount of published stories and cookbooks about ethnic foods has occurred in the past decade. These outpourings are reflected in the content of *Second Helpings*.

In reexamining the subject of food, many complex issues can be addressed. These topics include nutrition and diet, overeating, world hunger, and more equitable distribution of the world's food. *Second Helpings* does not set out to deal directly with these complicated issues but is sensitive to them and offers suggestions when appropriate for class discussion and student research. The script in chapter 8, "Out of the World's Breadbasket," entitled "Plenty to Go Around" is set in a part of eastern Africa where times have been hard and the animals are cautioned not to take more than their share, so there will be enough for all. Telling children multicultural stories and introducing food from around the world increases international understanding.

The scope of *Second Helpings'* food stories and activities is elementary school age children. This book is intended to be used as a resource book by teachers, librarians, and child care providers. It is literature based, annotating picture books published primarily after 1985. It also annotates selected longer books to be read aloud. The subtitle of *Mudluscious* identified a preschool audience, but that book can be used with children from preschool through third grade. This book does not target preschool children, but many of the activities can be adapted for an early childhood group.

A new feature for this book is the Starter Kit in each chapter. This kit introduces the theme with an appropriately related container. Thus, the eight chapters of this book are entitled: "Out of the Lunch Box" (lunch, picnics, and pizza); "Out of the Grocery Bag" (growing, shopping for food, and preparing food); "Out of the Giant Economy-size Trash Bag" (large quantities of food, big eaters, and fussy eaters); "Out of the Doggie Bag" (fun and fanciful food); "Out of the Carry-Out Box" (eating out and having dinner guests); "Out of the Cake Box" (bread and cakes, pies, cookies, ice cream, and sweets); "Out of the Soup Pot" (soups, stews, and leftovers); "Out of the World's Breadbasket" (food around the world).

The chapters are arranged in parallel fashion. After an introduction to the theme, the chapters continue with a focus book, activities that relate directly to the focus book, a longer book to be read aloud, related picture book titles, an original story, a readers theatre script, activities that relate to the chapter topic, the starter kit, and recipes.

The Starter Kit serves several functions. The idea of looking inside a container is fun for kids and for the adults using the kit. The container with its contents is a ready-made display item with visual appeal. On a practical side, the teacher or librarian can fill the container with books, food, story props, and items that expand the topic. For example, in chapter 2, "Out of the Grocery Bag," the starter kit would be a paper grocery bag (or a recyclable canvas grocery bag) packed with gardening tools and seed packets, grocery lists and coupons, recipe cards, a copy of the focus book *Something Good*, fresh vegetables, and a few kitchen utensils such as a whisk and a spatula. Copies of recipes and the script along with writing activities are also included. The kit itself can then be given to a group of children for small group work, making it a self-contained self-starter.

Each chapter includes a complete original readers theatre script to use with children in libraries and classrooms. Readers theatre is an increasingly popular way to share a story with immediate audience participation. In readers theatre the participants read from scripts rather than memorize lines as in a play. Minimal props, costumes, and movement are needed. For more background about readers theatre consult Caroline Feller Bauer's *Presenting Reader's Theater* (Wilson 1987).

Related Activities includes a few songs, poems, action rhymes, and chants. There are more opportunities for writing and speaking activities created by students themselves. Craft projects and games do not appear as a separate section; rather, they are integrated with the related activities. For example, students are encouraged to design and create their own menus, a project that would involve art and writing.

The recipes that appeared in *Mudluscious* were adult directed, while the recipes in *Second Helpings* are intended for student use. The format of each of the recipe pages is patterned after a cookbook. Each page can be photocopied and three-hole punched to make cookbooks. A list of ingredients with specific quantities, and a step-by-step method appear for each recipe. Drawings will serve as a help to the student cook. This format is intended to teach children that the steps of measuring and preparing precede the enjoyment of eating food.

Emphasis has been placed on developing activities along curricular lines. Public librarians are becoming familiar with school curricula and are coordinating programs with schools. This book will encourage mutual reinforcement of planning and cooperation between schools and public libraries. Math skills are taught as students shop for food and measure ingredients. An example of a science tie-in is one of the focus book activities for *June 29, 1999* in chapter 3, "Out of the Giant Economy-size Trash Bag." Students are asked to write about the main character's science project after reading about its amazing results. Numerous social studies connections are suggested in chapter 8 "Out of the World's Breadbasket," such as creating a Native American food map, and making a world stew (which is also a writing and speaking activity). Language arts connections are, of course, primary; many opportunities for writing and speaking are suggested. This is a literature-based resource book, so all of these activities grow from the picture books listed in each chapter's Related Titles section.

At workshops and library programs since the publication of *Mudluscious*, we have found that the appetite for food books has not been satiated. People have asked for more, so here are our *Second Helpings*!

Our special thanks to Ann M., Ann S., Lynn S., Denise K., and Carol E., the friends, librarians, and teachers who have nourished the ideas in this book.

Chapter 1

Out of the Lunch Box

Introduction

There is nothing that is more a symbol of the back-to-school time of year than a new lunch box. As trivial as this may seem to an adult, choosing between a lunch box with a super hero and one with a cartoon character may be very important to children who are just learning to make decisions on their own. For many children lunch is the first meal they will share regularly with people outside their families. The kinds of food make a lunch different from the rural midday meal, which is more like a traditional dinner. Lunch foods for kids should be foods they enjoy, like hot dogs, pizza, sandwiches, picnic food, chicken legs, and deviled eggs!

These informal meals appeal to children as a fun alternative to the traditional around-the-table family dinner. An example is the portable finger food that comes in small containers, often opened right at the table to reveal surprises. Another appeal is the sense of eating on the go, the independence in deciding where and how to eat. Some of the rules are suspended and everyone is more relaxed.

A special kind of lunch, or supper, is the picnic. This out-of-doors meal has such appeal that many books are written about it and many activities grow out of it. Also within the scope of this chapter are other foods closely associated with lunch, but not limited to lunch, especially pizza.

New pizza books such as *How Pizza Came to Queens* and *Pizza Man* inform the reader about the history of pizza and the preparation of this popular food. Lunch time with the animals can be an opportunity for some silly situations such as *Lunch with Aunt Augusta, Feathers for Lunch;* and Denise Fleming's *Lunch.* Dick Gackenbach's *Claude Has a Picnic,* several illustrated versions of the *Teddy Bear's Picnic,* and Anna Grossnickle Hines' *The Greatest Picnic in the World* represent the wide range of books on picnics enjoyed by animals and people.

How Pizza Came to Queens was selected as the focus book of the chapter because it is a highly plausible story that gives an historical context for a food that today is quite commonplace to the United States, but forty years ago was totally unknown to New York. Because the children shop for the pizza ingredients in this story, the related activities ask children to create shopping lists and research the library for pizza recipes and other foods. Social studies units can make use of *How Pizza Came to Queens* in its historical context.

1

Focus Book

How Pizza Came to Queens, by Dayal Kaur Khalsa. Clarkson N. Potter, 1989.

When Mrs. Pelligrino comes from Italy to visit May's town, she brings a strange green package and says sadly, "no pizza." May and her friends try to cheer up the woman, but finally discover she wants ingredients to make pizza, a dish unfamiliar at that time in Queens, New York. The girls shop and bring home the ingredients. Now Mrs. Pelligrino takes her rolling pin out of the green package, and begins to make the pizza. She is happy and makes pizza every day until her stay ends, leaving her legacy of pizza with the family.

Focus Book Activities

Spoken and Written Expression

The children in the book try many ways to make Mrs. Pelligrino happy before they find out she wants to make pizza. Brainstorm other things children might do to make a guest feel at home. List these on the chalkboard.

Written Expression

Make a shopping list of actual ingredients and amounts needed to make a pizza for a family or for the entire class. This activity will involve some research of cookbooks as well as math skills.

Written Expression

This book does not include a pizza recipe at the end, but students might enjoy writing a pizza story with Mrs. Pelligrino's family recipe at the end. Have students make up their own pizza recipes or research cookbooks to find good pizza recipes. This activity will involve learning that recipes are usually written with step-by-step instructions.

Spoken Expression

The children in this story put on a play to try to cheer up Mrs. Pelligrino. Have students make up a brief play or skit that the children of *How Pizza Came to Queens* could enact for Mrs. Pelligrino.

Written Expression

Have children write stories about how pizza might have come to your town. Create another character (rather than Mrs. Pelligrino) who comes to visit. Have this character tell her or his story.

Spoken Expression

Khalsa's illustrations provide many details about the historical period of this story. After you read the story, go through each picture with the students and have them say what looks different from today's world. What looks the same?

Spoken Expression

When the children first read about pizza in the library, they think it sounds strange. Ask children to tell about foods they thought sounded unappealing at first but later learned to like.

Spoken Expression

This story seems to be a family story. Most families have at least one treasured food story they share. Have children tell favorites.

Longer Read Aloud Book

Hiser, Constance. *No Bean Sprouts, Please.* Simon and Schuster, 1989. 57 pages.

James' mother is a nutrition nut, so no one will swap lunch items with him. Who wants to trade for a bean sprout sandwich? Then James' uncle sends him a new lunch box. Mom puts in bean sprouts, but at lunch time a chili dog and chips are in the box!

Related Titles

Barbour, Karen. *Little Nino's Pizzeria.* Harcourt Brace Jovanovich, 1987.

Tony enjoys helping his dad operate Little Nino's, a successful, small pizza restaurant. But when the father opens a fancy, expensive restaurant, no one has fun. In the end changing back to the smaller restaurant restores the family's pride and enjoyment.

Caines, Janette. *I Need a Lunch Box.* Illustrated by Pat Cummings. Harper & Row, 1988.

A little boy relates all the wonderful things his sister gets in preparation for going to first grade: a pencil case, an umbrella and raincoat, and a lunch box. The boy begins to dream of having five lunch boxes of different colors, one for each day of the school week. Pat Cummings exuberant illustrations of this African-American boy and his family and the lunch box decorations are made from stamp pad art created especially for this book.

Clark, Emma Chichester. *Lunch with Aunt Augusta.* Dial, 1991.

Hubert, Gerald, and Jemima, three young lemurs, have lunch with their Aunt Augusta. Jemima eats so much that she falls from the trees on their journey home. A bunch of friendly fruit bats carry her home and the parent lemurs reward them with fruit drinks.

Cocca-Leffer, Maryann. *Wednesday Is Spaghetti Day.* Scholastic, 1990.

Wednesday is just another day for the Tremante family but their cat Catrina waits impatiently until they all leave because then her friends come to make a glorious spaghetti lunch. They lose track of the time and dash to clean up just as the kids step off the school bus at three o'clock. The cats look forward to Thursday, at Ruby's—Guacamole Day.

Ehlert, Lois. *Feathers for Lunch.* Harcourt Brace Jovanovich, 1990.

With clear pictures and simple text, this story tells about a cat trying to catch birds for lunch. Each bird is carefully drawn and labeled. The cat keeps trying but his bell gives him away and the birds escape. The last pages show each bird again with some facts about its size, food, and home.

Fleming, Denise. *Lunch*. Henry Holt, 1992.

A little mouse eats his way through many colorful foods: purple grapes, red apples, and a pink watermelon—black seeds and all! The mouse enjoys his lunch enormously and is all full, until it is time for dinner.

Gackenbach, Dick. *Claude Has a Picnic*. Clarion, 1993.

Claude the dog visits his neighbors who seem bored or discontent. He manages to get all of them together; they share their extra hot dogs, corn on the cob, assorted pets, and games and have a most enjoyable picnic.

Hines, Anna Grossnickle. *The Greatest Picnic in the World*. Clarion, 1991.

Buddy and his mother prepare a wonderful picnic of such treats as turkey sandwiches, chocolate chip cookies, celery sticks, grape and raspberry drinks, apples, and eggs in this story written in rhyme. They even add a box full of assorted toys and supplies for Buddy's baby brother, taking much time getting ready. When rain spoils their original plans, they have the picnic inside.

Kennedy, Jimmy. *Teddy Bear's Picnic*. Illustrated by Prue Theobalds. Peter Bedrick, 1992.

The words to the traditional song are portrayed with a watercolor illustration of the sumptuous feast for the picnic. Picnic hampers are filled with jam and bread; baskets and fancy tablecloths display tea sandwiches, cakes, and sweets. The setting appears to be an English woodland.

Kennedy, James. *Teddy Bear's Picnic*. Illustrated by Renate Kozikowski. Aladdin Books, 1989.

The familiar day of games and treats in the woods for good little Teddy Bears is presented in a new way. Half-page cutouts allow each page to have an overlay that makes a new picture on the same background. The bears wear sneakers and cute clothes and really frolic until they are tired little teddy bears.

Kessler, Ethel and Leonard Kessler. *Stan the Hot Dog Man*. Harper & Row, 1992.

Stan retires from his job at the bakery and becomes a hot dog man with his own truck. The new job enables him to help children who are stranded in a snowstorm. Stan not only keeps them warm in his truck but he keeps them well-fed with his hot dogs.

Kovalski, Maryanne. *Pizza for Breakfast*. Morrow, 1991.

When Frank and Zelda's pizza business declines, a man grants them their every wish. Wishing for more customers, they get a lot; some even want pizza for breakfast. They add more staff and a bigger restaurant, but Frank and Zelda are stressed more than before. When the magic man appears again, they make a wish to have life the way it was, and they are content.

Krensky, Stephen. *The Pizza Book*. Illustrated by R. W. Alley. Scholastic, 1992.

In this story a father and daughter make a pizza. The history of pizza is related with several stories tucked inside. Fascinating facts are included (pizza made with red tomatoes, green basil, and white mozzarella was created for Queen Marghenta of Italy because the Italian flag is red, green, and white). Recipes are also included.

Martino, Teresa. *Pizza*. Illustrated by Brigid Faranda. Steck-Vaughn, 1992.

This book for the beginning reader sketches the history and preparation of pizza.

MacLean, Bill. *The Best Peanut Butter Sandwich in the Whole World.* Illustrated by Katherine Helmer. Black Moss Press, 1990.

When Billy sets out to get the ingredients for the best peanut butter sandwich in the whole world, he sparks the interest of the baker, the dairy clerk, and the health food store clerk. They come to his house and enjoy a sandwich for lunch.

Munsch, Robert. *Moira's Birthday.* Illustrated by Michael Martchenko. Annick, 1987.

Moira invites her whole school to her birthday party, despite her parents' wishes. This resourceful girl comes up with more than enough food, cakes, and pizza to share.

Pillar, Marjorie. *Pizza Man.* Crowell, 1990.

Photographs follow a pizza through all the stages of its preparation. The pizza man enjoys his work—and watching people eat it.

Pinczes, Elinor. *100 Hungry Ants.* Illustrated by Bonnie Mackain. Houghton Mifflin, 1993.

In a single-file line of 100 hungry ants, one declares that they are traveling much too slowly to get to a picnic and that the food will likely be gone by the time they arrive. They decide to travel more efficiently—in two lines of 50, then in four lines of 25, then in five lines of 20, and finally, in 10 lines of 10. When they arrive and the food is gone, 99 of the ants turn on the one who complained that they took too much time forming lines.

Related Activities

Pizza on a Roll

Make stick puppets for the following characters: Gennaro, a sugar cookie, an oatmeal cookie, a gingersnap, a cow, and farmers. Hold up the puppets as the characters are mentioned. Give several children sunglasses and have them act the parts of the teenagers. Make the pizza out of a large round circle of posterboard, attach it to the end of a dowel rod with a small nail, and spin it as you tell the story.

One year Gennaro's Pizzeria wanted to celebrate Columbus Day in a really big way. Gennaro took out an ad in the local newspaper to attract the public. The ad read: "World's Biggest Pizza Made Right Before Your Very Eyes. Come help out and have a free slice! October 12—Columbus Day—Dawn till Dusk."

So Gennaro assembled the ingredients. In the parking lot of the pizzeria Gennaro set out washtubs of water and yeast, salt and oil. He rented cement mixers to hold 100 pounds of flour and mix that up with the other ingredients.

Anyone who wanted a piece of pizza had to help knead the dough. So grandmas and grandpas, tots and teens all came to knead and knead and knead.

After three hours, Gennaro directed his cooks to spread all the tablecloths from the pizzeria on the tops of the washtubs that held the yeasty dough.

And then everyone waited for the dough to rise. Fortunately, it was a warm October day, so the pizza dough got bigger and bigger and bigger.

By noon the pizza was big enough to take out of the tubs and roll out. Where would they roll out all that pizza dough?

Well, Gennaro had asked the street department to scrub down the parking lot. Then he had the cement mixers sprinkle more flour on the pavement. Now everyone lifted an armful of pizza dough onto the parking lot. And everyone stretched and pulled that pizza until it was monstrous! The day got so hot that the monstrous pizza baked right there in the sun.

And surely that would have been the biggest pizza in town. But then a very strange thing happened. No one knew why. Perhaps too much yeast had been added. Or maybe the sun spots produced a chemical reaction with the yeast. Or maybe a tropical storm set the world off balance. Whatever happened, it caused that pizza dough to start rolling around all by itself.

"Come back here you monster pizza!" shouted Gennaro. "We made you, and now we want to eat you!"

But the pizza was on a roll now and had no intention of stopping, so it just kept right on rolling. And as it rolled, it sang out: "I'm a pizza on a roll, rolling and all hot to go! You can't make me settle down. I am rolling out of town. I'm a pizza on a roll, rolling and all hot to go!"

The monster pizza rolled past the bakery. Inside the bakery were dozens of cookies.

One sugar cookie turned to an oatmeal and said, "This story sounds familiar. Didn't our cousin the gingerbread boy do something like this last year?"

"Perhaps we should stop the pizza before it creates any trouble," said the oatmeal cookie.

"Oh be quiet," snapped the gingersnap. "Just let him find out for himself."

So the monster pizza rolled on past the bakery, past the dairy, and out into the country.

"Come back here you monster pizza," called out a cow. "You look even better than that gingerbread boy who came by here last year. I want to eat you!"

But the pizza was on a roll now and had no intention of stopping, so it just kept right on rolling. And as it rolled, it sang out: "I'm a pizza on a roll, rolling and all hot to go! You can't make me settle down. I am rolling out of town. I'm a pizza on a roll, rolling and all hot to go!"

Before long the monster pizza came to a field and farmers harvesting corn. "Come back here you monster pizza," they all called. "We couldn't catch that gingerbread boy who came through here last year. Now we're really hungry. We want to eat you!"

But the pizza was on a roll now and had no intention of stopping, so it just kept right on rolling. And as it rolled, it sang out: "I'm a pizza on a roll, rolling and all hot to go! You can't make me settle down. I am rolling out of town. I'm a pizza on a roll, rolling and all hot to go!"

The pizza rolled and rolled until it came to the ocean. There on the beach were a bunch of teenagers. They called out, "Hey! We're hungry! We want to eat you!"

But the pizza was on a roll now and had no intention of stopping, so it just kept right on rolling. And as it rolled, it sang out: "I'm a pizza on a roll, rolling and all hot to go! You can't make me settle down. I am rolling out of town. I'm a pizza on a roll, rolling and all hot to go!"

But the pizza had met his match. For there is nothing on this earth that can escape a group of hungry teenagers, not even a monster pizza on a roll. The teenagers chased him faster and faster. The pizza was rolling faster than he had ever rolled, so fast that the world began to spin around.

"Hey, pizza," a teenager called, "You are a fast, fine pizza. You can roll and roll. But can you spin?"

"Yea, like a giant CD?" called another. "Bet you can't spin like that."

"Yea, pizza, can you do that? Spin for us if you're so hot to go."

The pizza fell over on his crust and began to spin. "I can spin, I can spin. Watch this." And the pizza went spinning and spinning until it was so dizzy it wobbled to a halt. The teenagers caught it and gobbled it down.

Then one teenager said, "Hey, this was great. I don't even miss not catching that gingerbread kid last year!"

Picnic of Picnics

Characters

Aunt Annie
Aunt Barbie
Aunt Connie   } ants
Aunt Debbie
Aunt Ethel
Two Narrators

Stage setup: Arrange five chairs or stools in a line or semicircle; a narrator stands at each end, and the Aunts are seated with Aunt Ethel in the middle.

Readers theatre scripts are not meant to be memorized, but read with animation. After parts are assigned, let children read over the script to get a sense of the characters they will play. For the performance, children can stand or be seated on stools. Occasionally, a character moves from one place to another (this is indicated in the script), but, in general, characters use body language to express emotions and action. For this script, characters can turn away from the audience when they are not involved.

Costumes in readers theatre are minimal, but, in this script, black pipe-cleaner antennae would be fun. Mount the antennae on headbands so they can wiggle without falling off.

Narrator 1: There was once a colony of ants that gathered every Wednesday for a quilting bee.

Narrator 2: The first Wednesday of July happened to be the Fourth of July, so the ants called off the quilting bee and planned a picnic.

Aunt Annie: We'll meet by the sweet-gum tree and each bring something for a picnic.

Aunt Barbie: Good idea! I'll bring the brownies.

Aunt Connie: No, I'll bring the brownies.

Aunt Debbie: But I make the best brownies.

Aunt Ethel: Oh, clam up. There must be 100 picnics in the park on the Fourth of July. Let's each pick a different picnic and help ourselves. Then we can share everything we get.

Narrator 1: So that was the plan.

Narrator 2: On the Fourth of July Aunt Annie set out first.

Aunt Annie: Look at that! A big wicker picnic basket. I'll bet there's a real traditional home-style picnic in that basket. I hope they open it up soon so I can take a peek. Oh, goody! That little kid's got the top open to get some potato chips. I'll just wiggle on over and climb in. Mmmm. Hot dogs. Hamburgers. And potato salad. I'll just have a little of everything.

Narrator 1: So that is what Aunt Annie did. Next, Aunt Barbie set out for another area of the park.

Aunt Barbie: Wow! What a sleek cooler. That family must be upscale. Oh, yummy, they've opened it to get out the mineral water. I'll just sneak over and have a look. Mmmm. Pâté. Brie cheese. Strawberries dipped in dark chocolate. I'll just have a little of everything.

Narrator 2: And that is what Aunt Barbie did. In another part of the park, Aunt Connie found a picnic she liked.

Aunt Connie: My oh my. I just love fried chicken. And the smell of fried chicken is coming out of that food hamper. What else is in that Southern picnic? My oh my. They can't resist it either—someone's sneaking a chicken leg. Mmmm. Fried chicken. Biscuits. Pecan pie. I'll just have a little of everything.

Narrator 1: So that is what Aunt Connie did. Nearby, Aunt Debbie spied another picnic.

Aunt Debbie: A picnic in a pot? What kind of food do they have? Oh, good, someone is opening it to stir the pot. Mmmm. A mess of clams, and corn on the cob, and a whole lobster! This must be a New England clambake. I'll just have a little of everything.

Narrator 2: And Aunt Debbie brought back good things for the picnic. The last ant to go out was Aunt Ethel. She found a picnic already in progress.

Aunt Ethel: This group brought everything and the kitchen sink. Well, if they didn't bring the sink, they brought their own grill. They are cooking barbecue right out here. Mmmm. Barbecue ribs and barbecue chicken. And lots of beans. I'll just have a little of everything.

Narrator 1: So Aunt Ethel took her food back to the sweet-gum tree where the others were waiting.

Aunt Annie: Here's what I brought from a traditional picnic. Good old family fare. Hot dogs and hamburgers.

Aunt Barbie: Mine's really upscale. Pâté and strawberries dipped in chocolate.

Aunt Connie: Make mine Southern fry. Chicken, of course. And pecan pie.

Aunt Debbie: Here's a real nice clambake from New England.

Aunt Ethel: Howdy. I'm bringing you Texas barbecue.

Narrator 2: Well, this was the picnic of picnics!

Narrator 1: And to top it all off, Aunt Ethel brought dessert.

Aunt Ethel: You bet I did. My very own homemade brownies.

Other Activities

Sandwich Spread on a Bread Chant

This chant can be shared, as it is written here, with younger children. They will enjoy clapping out the rhythm, and this will develop their musical appreciation and prepare them to better understand the musical rhythms of language patterns.

Older children will be inspired to create their own verses to add to this chant. Notice that for each stanza, most of the lines are repeated and only the food varies . Older children may create their own stanzas that use a repeated rhyme scheme such as the one suggested here.

Make a sandwich Here's the bread Tell me what's next For the spread? Chicken salad For my lunch Add a big gob Ready? Munch!	Make a sandwich Here's the bread Tell me what's next For the spread? Ham and more ham For my lunch Add a big gob Ready? Munch!
Make a sandwich Here's the bread Tell me what's next For the spread? Peanut butter For my lunch Add a big gob Ready? Munch!	Make a sandwich Here's the bread Tell me what's next For the spread? Cherry jelly For my lunch Add a big gob Ready? Munch!

Ask the children if that's all they want to suggest and then have them all chorus, "Yum! You all come!"

M-m-m-m! Good!

Begin by brainstorming and listing jingles and slogans the children know, such as "No one can eat just one" and "It's the real thing." In general, a jingle features one trait of the food and puts it in a context that sounds fun and up-to-date.

Now take some less famous foods and make jingles and slogans to promote them. For example, a popcorn slogan could be "Keeps us hoppin' when it's poppin'." After that, see if you can write jingles for items on the school lunch menu!

Wanna Trade?

You may sing the first verse to the tune of "Did You Ever See a Lassie." To allow children the freedom to be creative when naming food, don't force the meter in the other verses.

Oh, what's inside your lunch box,
your lunch box, your lunch box?
Oh, what's inside your lunch box?
Do you want to trade?

There's pickles and peppers,
And pizza and pastrami.
Oh, what's inside your lunch box?
Do you want to trade?

There's melons and mashed potatoes
And marshmallows and matzo balls.
Oh, what's inside your lunch box?
Do you want to trade?

Each child chooses four foods that begin with the same letter to add verses to this rhyme. For older children, challenge them to write 26 verses, one for each letter!

Starter Kit

The "Out of the Lunch Box" Starter Kit will provide a visual aid that will introduce your food theme or unit quickly. No one can resist wondering what is inside a bag or basket, so just setting it on a display or holding it up will attract attention. The items inside the container will introduce the "flavor" of the food theme and start imaginations racing. In addition, many of the items will be used in specific activities or stories, so it is easy for you to assemble. It's all in the bag!

For this lunch-and-picnic theme, you might pack these items into a colorful lunch box or a big picnic basket with smaller lunch boxes inside:

plaid picnic tablecloth
food slogans from magazines
plastic pizza to roll for the story "Pizza on a Roll"
six headbands with black antennas attached and a copy of the script "Picnic of
    Picnics"
copy of the focus book *How Pizza Came to Queens*
cassette recording of *Teddy Bear's Picnic* to use with the books
frozen-pizza box
assortment of lunch bags, small brown bags
transparency of "Sandwich Spread on a Bread Chant"

Also for this theme, you might develop individual lunch boxes containing cards for small groups to write verses for the "Wanna Trade?" activity.

Recipes

Deviled Eggs

INGREDIENTS:

6 EGGS
1 TABLESPOON MayoNNaise
½ Teaspoon MUSTARD
1 Teaspoon PICKLe ReLISH

METHOD:

DEVILED EGGS

1. Place eggs in a Pan and cover them with Cold water.
2. Place pan over medium heat and let water boil. Turn down heat until it bubbles gently. Let cook about 15 minutes.
3. Remove Pan from heat and run cold water over the eggs. Set aside until they are cool.
4. Shell eggs and slice into halves.
5. Take out the egg yolks and smash with a fork.
6. Mix egg yolks with mayonnaise, mustard, and relish. Spoon this mixture back into the hollow of the egg white halves.

From *Second Helpings*. Copyright © 1994. Teacher Ideas Press, P.O. Box 6633, Englewood, CO 80155-6633, 1-800-237-6124.

Chicken Legs

InGReDieNTS:
6 CHICKEN LEGS
½ CUP SOUR CREAM
¼ CUP MARGARINE
1 CUP BREAD CRUMBS
1 TABLESPOON GRATED PARMESAN CHEESE
SALT, PEPPER, PAPRIKA to TASTE

METHOD:

CHICKEN LEGS

1. MELT MARGARINE in a DISH in a MICROWAVE or in a PAN on the STOVE.
2. DIP CHICKEN LEGS in MARGARINE and BRUSH the SOUR CREAM OVER THEM.
3. MIX TOGETHER the BREAD CRUMBS, PARMESAN CHEESE, SALT, PEPPER, and PAPRIKA.
4. ROLL the CHICKEN LEGS in THIS MIXTURE.
5. PLACE CHICKEN LEGS on a BAKING SHEET or in a SHALLOW BAKING PAN.
6. BAKE for ONE HOUR in a 350 DEGREE OVEN.

Pizza Sandwiches

INGREDIENTS:

2 ENGLISH MUFFIN HALVES (1 BUN OR 1 BAGEL) FOR EACH PERSON
1 TABLESPOON SAUCE FOR EACH SANDWICH
1 SLICE OF CHEESE FOR EACH SANDWICH
1 SLICE OF GREEN PEPPER FOR EACH SANDWICH
4 SLICES OF PEPPERONI FOR EACH SANDWICH
1/4 TEASPOON OREGANO OR PARMESAN CHEESE FOR EACH SANDWICH

METHOD:

PIZZA SANDWICHES

1. HEAT OVEN TO 400 DEGREES.
2. CUT MUFFINS, BUNS, OR BAGELS INTO HALVES.
3. SPREAD SAUCE ON EACH SANDWICH HALF. (USE A LITTLE EXTRA IF YOU LIKE SAUCE!)
4. PLACE CHEESE SLICE ON TOP OF SAUCE.
5. SLICE GREEN PEPPER INTO THIN SLICES OR STRIPS.
6. PLACE GREEN PEPPER SLICE AND PEPPERONI SLICES ON TOP OF CHEESE.
7. SPRINKLE OREGANO OR PARMESAN CHEESE ON TOP OF THIS. (USE BOTH IF YOU LIKE!)
8. PLACE SANDWICHES OPEN FACED ON COOKIE SHEET AND BAKE FOR 10 MINUTES OR UNTIL CHEESE MELTS.
9. EAT YOUR SANDWICH OPEN FACED OR PUT THE TWO HALVES TOGETHER, SO YOU CAN HAVE YOUR PIZZA ON THE GO!

Chapter 2

Out of the Grocery Bag

Introduction

The scope of this chapter is broad and includes the topics of growing food, shopping for food, preparing food, and nutritional foods. Although not many picture story books about nutritional foods exist, there are interesting nonfiction resource books available for children. Lerner/Carolrhoda have several series of high-quality books about food and nutrition. These are listed in the Resource Bibliography.

Children take their first shopping trips in baby carriers. Wise parents use these as learning experiences. There are opportunities for talking about food choices and the ways in which foods are organized in a store, and simply naming the different foods that exist. Having a garden and learning where food comes from can be important educational experiences for young children. Preparing food teaches skills of measuring, sequencing, and counting; following a recipe teaches basic reading skills.

Sharing in the process of food preparation is an opportunity to teach responsibility. In much of the world, the preparation of food is still strictly a woman's activity. In the United States, with so many single-parent families and families with two working parents, the kitchen is no longer solely the domain of the female or mother. Both boys and girls are learning more about food preparation and learning to share this role.

There are a number of books on gardening, from *Growing Vegetable Soup* to *Happy Veggies*, books for very young gardeners. Slightly older children will enjoy *Green Beans* and *Johnny Appleseed*. Preparing for dinner can be as fun as Susanna Gretz's *It's Your Turn, Roger;* dads as well as moms take part in Anna Hines' *Daddy Makes the Best Spaghetti.*

The focus book *Something Good*, by Robert Munsch, portrays grocery store shopping as outlandish, with exaggeration, and from the different points of view of a parent and a child considering what is "good." A "good" writing activity growing from this book has students make up two shopping lists, one for father and one for child.

Science and math skills develop from the books and activities in this chapter. Students will be introduced to natural science through reading *Growing Vegetable Soup* and will want to grow their own vegetables. Examining food prices, suggested in the activity "Don't Forget the . . . ," will teach basic math skills. Reading food labels, an activity related to the Focus Book *Something Good*, will show even reluctant readers that reading is a key to learning.

Focus Book

Something Good, by Robert Munsch. Illustrated by Michael Martchenko. Annick Press, 1990.

Tyya goes shopping with her father, brother, and sister, but she has different ideas from her father about what "good" things they should buy at the store. When her father tells her to not move, she gets into even more trouble. In the end, the father and the daughter agree on what is "something good."

Focus Book Activities

Spoken Expression

Bob Munsch's book reads very well aloud. Change this picture book into a story that the teacher or a student can tell to the class.

Spoken Expression

Change the book into a readers theatre script with different children reading and acting out the parts.

Written and Spoken Expression

Have the class make a list of all the things that happen after Father tells Tyya to stand still in the store. Students dictate this list to the teacher who writes it on the chalkboard.

Written Expression

This is a story about two different points of view about what are "good" foods. Make up one shopping list for the father and one for Tyya.

Spoken Expression

Most children have shopped in a grocery store with a parent. Encourage children to tell about something funny or upsetting that happened to them in a grocery.

Spoken Expression

Grocery shopping often involves reading labels. Have children study labels on packaged foods and tell the class what they learned.

Longer Read Aloud Book

Corbett, Scott. *The Lemonade Trick.* Illustrated by Paul Galdone. Scholastic, 1960. 103 pages.

Kerby is not a bad kid, but the chemical lemonade he mixes and drinks makes him too good to be true. And when the lemonade goodness wears off, watch out!

Related Titles

Ehlert, Lois. *Growing Vegetable Soup*. Harcourt Brace Jovanovich, 1987.

Simple text and intensely bright pictures tell the story of a young child and a father growing vegetables and making soup.

Florian, Douglas. *A Chef*. Greenwillow, 1992.

Part of the series How We Work. A female chef shops for ingredients and prepares a wide variety of foods for a restaurant. Going through a chef's day will give children much information about this occupation.

Florian, Douglas. *Vegetable Garden*. Harcourt Brace Jovanovich, 1991.

Sparse text in verse and watercolor illustrations tell of a family planting and harvesting a garden.

Gretz, Susanna. *It's Your Turn, Roger*. Dial, 1985.

When Roger Pig feels put upon to help prepare dinner, he goes to the neighbors' to be a "guest." After being invited to eat various strange foods, he smells home cooking and decides it is worth the work, especially when there is worm pie for dessert!

Grossman, Bill. *Tommy at the Grocery Store*. Illustrated by Victoria Chess. Harper & Row, 1989.

Tommy Pig is left at the grocery store and customers, seeing only parts of his body (such as his neck), think he is a grocery item (a bottle with a long neck) and purchase him. Written in hysterical rhyme, poor Tommy is mistaken for meat, potatoes, a bottle, corn, and a table. Each time the customer returns unwanted Tommy. Finally his mother sees all of him at once and takes him home.

Hines, Anna. *Daddy Makes the Best Spaghetti*. Houghton Mifflin, 1976.

After day care, Corey and daddy buy the ingredients and prepare spaghetti before mom comes home. Mom pronounces it "especially good!"

Hutchins, Pat. *Don't Forget the Bacon*. William Morrow, 1976.

A boy's mental grocery list gets scrambled and unscrambled, but he still forgets the bacon!

Kellogg, Steven. *Chicken Little*. William Morrow, 1985.

Chicken Little thinks the sky is falling when hit by an acorn. Friends gather to help, including Lucy Goosey and Turkey Lurkey. Finally, Fox arrives with lots of good recipes—for a fowl dinner. Help arrives in a helicopter, and Chicken Little lives to see the mighty oak tree grow from the original acorn.

Kellogg, Steven. *Johnny Appleseed*. Morrow, 1988.

As America spreads west, John Chapman sees the need for fruit trees—apple trees, to be specific. He is a peaceful man who wears a pot for a hat and has bare feet. The stories people make up after meeting Johnny Appleseed add to his fame. This is the true story of John Chapman's life, enhanced enormously by Kellogg's fanciful and charming illustrations.

Koscielniak, Bruce. *Bear and Bunny Grow Tomatoes*. Knopf, 1993.

Bear and Bunny both plant tomatoes, but while Bear works hard, Bunny takes lazy short cuts. They both end up with a good harvest because of Bear's bumper crop and generosity.

Nordqvist, Sven. *Pancake Pie*. William Morrow, 1985.

Farmer Festus is determined to make a delicious pancake pie for his cat Mercury's birthday, but he has to overcome many difficulties in order to get the ingredients.

Oda, Mayumi. *Happy Veggies*. Parallax Press, 1986.

This brief text celebrates the growth of vegetables in a garden—with the flowing brush stroke paintings of an internationally renowned artist.

Oxenbury, Helen. *Tom and Pippo Go Shopping*. Aladdin Books, 1988.

Tom gets samples of bread, fruit, and cheese at the grocery store by saying his stuffed monkey wants a taste. He eats them himself.

Robbins, Ken. *Make Me a Peanut Butter Sandwich (and a Glass of Milk)*. Scholastic, 1992.

Photographs take the reader step by step from farm (and cow) to snack on the table.

Thomas, Elizabeth. *Green Beans*. Illustrated by Vicki Jo Redenbaugh. Carolrhoda, 1992.

Gramma is upset when her green beans don't grow in the garden. When she goes on vacation the green beans flourish so the family has more than enough for a green bean feast.

Thompson, Peggy. *Siggy's Spaghetti Works*. Illustrated by Gloria Kamen. William Morrow, 1993.

Siggy loves to make spaghetti, about 100 tons each day in his factory. This tour of the spaghetti plant shows dough becoming pasta as Siggy describes the history of this popular food.

Williams, Vera. *Cherries and Cherry Pits*. Morrow, 1986.

Bidemmi draws and tells stories. In the first few stories she tells about different people sharing cherries and spitting out the pits. Then she draws a self-portrait where she saves the pits to plant a cherry tree. Soon, real cherry trees are everywhere in the neighborhood.

Related Activities

In Good Shape

Draw and Tell Story

Use a chalkboard or markers and paper to draw this story as you tell it. (The accompanying drawings appear in the appendix on page 136.) Follow the instructions for drawing lines as they appear in the story. How soon will the children realize what you are drawing? Encourage their participation. Increase their memory skills by asking questions about the items Willy must get at the grocery store.

Willy was having a party on Friday night. He had done most of the shopping earlier in the week, but on the way home from work he had to pick up a few things. He made a list.

    bratwurst
    pickles
    ginger ale
    taco chips
    jelly beans
    rocky road ice cream
    pretzels

Willy said to himself, I'll just pick up these seven things and I'll be in good shape.

Willy left work and drove to the supermarket. But just as he got inside he realized the list was at home on the kitchen counter. How could he remember the foods without the list? Willy thought, Let's see. There was something I was going to cook on the grill and serve on a bun. He headed to the meat department. (Draw line 1.) What do you think he got there? (Bratwurst)

Right. He got bratwurst. Willy said to himself, I'll just pick up these six things and I'll be in good shape. Then Willy had to think again. There was something green and bumpy and very crunchy. He headed to the relish department. (Draw line 2.) What do you think he got there? (Pickles)

Right. He got pickles. Willy said to himself, I'll just pick up these five things and I'll be in good shape. Then Willy had to think again. There was something to drink that tickles the nose with its bubbles. He headed to the beverage department. (Draw line 3.) What do you think he got there? (Ginger ale)

Right. He got ginger ale. Willy said to himself, I'll just pick up these four things and I'll be in good shape. Then Willy had to think again. There was something salty and spicy and extra, extra crunchy. He headed to the snack foods department. (Draw line 4.) What do you think he got there? (Taco chips)

Right. He got taco chips. Willy said to himself, I'll just pick up these three things and I'll be in good shape. Then Willy had to think again. There was something sweet and chewy and it comes in lots of colors. He headed to the candy department. (Draw line 5.) What do you think he got there? (Jelly beans)

Right. He got jelly beans. Willy said to himself, I'll just pick up these two things and I'll be in good shape. Then Willy had to think again. There was something cold and gooey and yummy-yummy. He headed to the frozen food case. (Draw line 6.) What do you think he got there? (Rocky road ice cream)

Right. He got rocky road ice cream. But that was all Willy could remember. He had been all over the store and had gotten

    bratwurst
    pickles
    ginger ale
    taco chips
    jelly beans
    rocky road ice cream

What else was Willy supposed to get? (Show the completed drawing of the pretzel.)

Right! Pretzels! Willy said, I should have remembered pretzels all along. They are the best shape and now I am in good shape for this party!

Peter Pepper's Pickle Patch

Characters:

Peter Pepper
Earl April
Garden Storekeeper
Narrator

Stage setup: Arrange three chairs or stools in a line or semicircle and seat the narrator at one end.

Readers theatre scripts are not meant to be memorized, but read with animation. After parts are assigned, let children read over the script to get a sense of the characters they will play. For the performance, children can stand or be seated on stools. Occasionally, a character moves from one place to another (this is indicated in the script), but, in general, characters use body language to express emotions and action. For extra fun have children make pickle finger puppets from green construction paper so they can wiggle the pickles when they grow out of the garden in the story.

Narrator: Once upon a time there was a lad named Peter Pepper. Peter Pepper was a fine lad, but he was a little bit forgetful.

Peter: Hi! You may have heard of my uncle. His name is Peter Piper. He's the Peter Piper who picked a peck of———oh dear, let me see if I can remember what Peter Piper picked. Does anyone know what Peter Piper picked a peck of?

Narrator: Please, Peter, we'll never get on with this story!

Peter: Sorry.

Narrator: Once, Peter Pepper decided he wanted to grow a patch of pickles. So he went to the garden store to buy a pack of pickle seeds.

Peter: Please, Mr. Earl April, do you have any pickle seeds?

Earl April: Pickle seeds? I have never heard of such a silly thing.

Peter: Well, you've heard of pickles haven't you?

Earl April: Of course I have!

Peter: Then, do you have any pickle plants?

Earl April: Pickle plants? I have never heard of such a silly thing.

Peter: Please, do you know what I should do if I want to grow a patch of pickles?

Earl April: Any particular kind of pickles?

Peter: Yes! I prefer dill pickles.

Earl April: Well, why didn't you say so in the first place. Look, I have dill seeds. And I have cucumber seeds. If you plant these dill seeds next to these cucumber seeds by the pale moonlight and then laugh out loud three times, tickle your funny bone, and give your left leg a slap, you'll come up with dill pickles.

Peter: Oh my! I hope I can remember all that. Plant the dill next to the pickles. No, plant the dill next to the peppers. No, I've got it—plant the dill next to the cucumbers. Then you tickle your left leg, slap your funny bone and laugh out loud three times.

Earl April: Well, you're close. But maybe I'd better repeat the directions just one more time. Look, I have dill seeds. And I have cucumber seeds. If you plant these dill seeds next to these cucumber seeds by the pale moonlight and then laugh out loud three times, tickle your funny bone, and give your left leg a slap, you'll come up with dill pickles. Do you have that?

Peter: I think so.

Earl April: Good. Now, after the pickles start to pop up, get 16 silly kids to sing the pickle song with you while you pick the pickles in the pale moonlight. If you don't find 16 kids to sing, then the pickle patch will vanish. And you will have no pickles to pick. But if you do sing, you'll have so many pickles to pick that you will laugh yourself silly!

Peter: That sounds wonderful. I love pickles. And I love to laugh. But, please, could you teach me the pickle song?

Earl April: Oh, all right. I'll sing it one time, but you'd better listen hard so you will remember.

The Pickle Song
(Tune: "My Bonnie Lies Over the Ocean")

The pickles are growing this evening
Out in the pale moonlight
The pickles are growing this evening
Oh tell me the minute they're ripe.

Pick them, pick them
Pick them as quick as you can, you can
Pick them, pick them
Dill is my favorite brand!

Peter: Thanks, Mr. April. I'll try to remember all you've said.

Narrator: So Peter Pepper took his seeds home. By the pale moonlight, he sprinkled the dill seeds in one row of his garden, and he sprinkled the cucumber seeds in another row. Now, he had to do three more things. But poor Peter couldn't remember what three things he was supposed to do. Can anyone here help? (The Narrator gets answers from kids in audience. Motion to them if a prompt is needed.)

Narrator: Good—tickle your funny bone—slap your left leg—and laugh out loud three times.

Narrator: And before you could say Peter Pepper, dill pickles popped up out of Peter's garden. (Children raise their pickle puppets.)

Peter: Wow! Look at all these pickles growing in my garden patch! I can hardly wait to eat them!

Narrator: Wait a minute, Peter. Aren't you supposed to do something else?

Peter: That's right! I need 16 kids. Where can I find 16 kids? Do I have 16 kids out there who will help me sing the pickle song? Good! Now, everybody, sing your hearts out!

> The pickles are growing this evening
> Out in the pale moonlight
> The pickles are growing this evening
> Oh tell me the minute they're ripe.
> Pick them, pick them
> Pick them as quick as you can, you can
> Pick them, pick them
> Dill is my favorite brand!

Narrator: And, so, Peter Pepper's garden patch grew pecks and pecks of pickles. Dill pickles. His favorite kind. And Peter Pepper picked and picked and picked dill pickles until he laughed himself silly!

Other Activities

Smart Grocery Cart Chant

This chant can be shared, as it is written here, with younger children. Notice that children will suggest the food for the first line of each stanza and the next three lines never change. Clap out the rhythm so children will feel it in the language. This activity also helps develop an appreciation of musical rhythm.

After you introduce a model such as the one shown here, older children will enjoy creating their own verses. Use foods to teach the alphabet, foods in a particular category such as fruits and vegetables, or foods from a particular section of the grocery store.

> Got your list
> Aren't you smart?
> Tell me what
> Goes in the cart!
>
> Apples, apples
> Aren't you smart
> Tell me what
> Goes in the cart!

Don't Forget the ...

Develop a written version of a cumulative story by completing the sentence, "I'm going to the grocery store, and I don't want to forget———." You can develop this activity in several different ways.

Write the sentence at the top of a large sheet of paper. Children name food items from the store to make a list and then read aloud the entire list. After five or ten items, see if any individual child can name them all.

Let children copy the sentences on their own papers and make individual lists. Each child can be assigned a different letter of the alphabet to begin each food item listed. Or they can list a different food for each letter in their names.

These food lists can be used for a spelling bee or compiled into one master list. Introduce math by having children look in stores or ads for the prices of the different foods. Give bonus points to children who find coupons for the items on their lists!

Trip to the Store

We're going to the grocery store
Walk, walk, walk (*tap hands rhythmically on legs*)
    to the store
Door swings open all by itself (*put palms together in front of
    stomach, separate for "open," bring together for "closed"*)
    and closed
Open and closed
Open and closed
Oops, store manager is watching
Better start shopping
Walk, walk, walk (*tap hands rhythmically on legs*)
First go into fresh fruit
Get a grapefruit
Throw it up into the air (*pretend to toss ball in air*)
    and catch it when it comes down (*pretend to catch ball*)
Up and down
Up and down
Up and down
Oops, the store manager is watching
Better put it in the grocery cart
Walk, walk, walk (*tap hands rhythmically on legs*)
Over to the frozen food
Brrrrr (*shiver*)
Let's get ice cream and frozen pizza
Brrrrr
Hold the door open so the cold air comes out
Brrrrr

(Cumulative story continues on page 24.)

Oops, the store manager is watching
Better put these in the grocery cart
Walk, walk, walk (*tap hands rhythmically on legs*)
Here we are in canned goods
Let's stack them up (*pretend to stack cans*)
Corn on the bottom
     and then beans
     and then pineapple
     and then tuna
     and then sweet potatoes
     and then tomato sauce
     and then
          CRASH!

Oops! Here comes the store manager!
Put all the cans back
Tomato sauce (*pretend to pick up cans*)
Sweet potatoes
Tuna
Pineapple
Beans
Corn
RUN (*tap hands quickly on legs*)
    to the frozen foods
Brrrrr (*shiver*)
Put back the ice cream and the frozen pizza
RUN
Back to fresh fruit
Toss the grapefruit (*pretend to toss ball quickly*)
Up, Down, Up, Down, Up, Down
RUN (*tap hands quickly on legs*)
Back through the magic doors (*repeat open and close motion*)
Open and closed
Open, closed, open, closed
RUN (*tap hands quickly on legs*)
All the way home
and slam the door (*clap loudly*)
Now what will we eat? Let's order pizza (*hold hand like talking on the telephone*)
They deliver!

Step by Step

Children don't realize they use sequencing skills every day. Help them observe these skills closely by breaking a food preparation into steps. A good food to prepare is a peanut butter sandwich.

Number a large paper 1-10. Let one child suggest a step. Ask, "Does anything come before that?" For example, if a child says that one step is "get out bread," other children may answer your question by suggesting buying or baking bread. Carry the process as far back as the children can be directly involved. (You don't need to get into growing wheat and grinding flour.) This will be step number 1.

Now proceed through the steps of making the sandwich by asking, "What happens next?" List the steps as children mention them. If they jump a step, ask, "Does anything come before that?" You may have more than 10 steps. Use this master list in different ways.

Cut apart the steps and cut off the numbers. Now have children put the steps in order.

Write the steps on individual sheets of paper. Children can illustrate each step. Assemble the papers into a book.

Let children think of other types of food preparation to sequence. Heating canned soup, assembling a submarine sandwich, or making beef stew are all straightforward.

Starter Kit

The "Out of the Grocery Bag" Starter Kit will provide a visual aid that will introduce your food theme or unit quickly. No one can resist wondering what is inside a bag or basket, so just setting it on a display or holding it up will attract attention. The items inside the container will introduce the "flavor" of the food theme and start imaginations racing. In addition, many of the items will be used in specific activities or stories, so it is easy for you to assemble. It's all in the bag!

For this chapter's theme of growing, shopping for, and preparing food, you might pack these items into a paper or plastic grocery bag:

gardening tools
seed packs for fruits and vegetables
decorated grocery lists
recipe cards
coupons
large drawing paper for the story "In Good Shape"
pretzels for treats after reading the story "In Good Shape"
copy of the focus book *Something Good*
the book *A Chef,* for an overview of food preparation
fresh vegetables, and their more familiar canned counterparts
assorted kitchen utensils such as a whisk, different size spoons, a spatula, and pan-
     cake turners
giant veggies from someone's garden
aprons, hot pads, oven mitts, vegetable peeler, graters, and egg slicers
copy of the script "Peter Pepper's Pickle Patch"
copies of the recipe pages for each child

Recipes

Peter Rabbit Salads in a Cup

These two salads require no cooking (well, almost no cooking, if you have a hard-boiled egg ready in your refrigerator) and they can be taken along in their cups for your lunch. Teachers and parents will love the convenience. Besides, they're really healthy for kids and they taste good too.

Carrot Salad

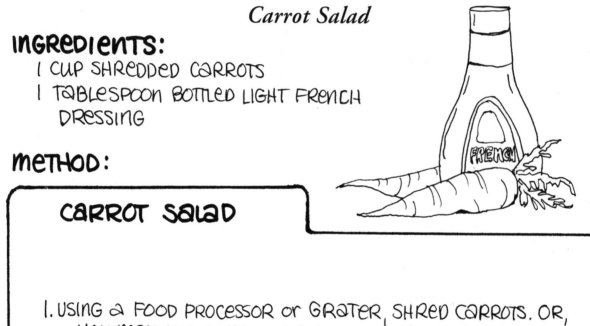

INGREDIENTS:
 1 CUP SHREDDED CARROTS
 1 TABLESPOON BOTTLED LIGHT FRENCH DRESSING

METHOD:

CARROT SALAD

1. USING a FOOD PROCESSOR or GRATER, SHRED CARROTS. OR, YOU MAY USE a VEGETABLE PEELER and MAKE CARROT CURLS. USE a PAPER PLATE for a WORK SURFACE.
2. SCOOP UP ONE CUP of the CARROTS and PUT in an empty PLASTIC YOGURT CUP.
3. POUR the FRENCH DRESSING OVER the CARROTS.

Sprout Surprise Salad

INGREDIENTS:

- ½ CUP alfalfa SPROUTS
- 2 SLICES of HARD-COOKED EGG
- 1 SLICE of CUCUMBER
- 1 TEASPOON of mayonnaise

METHOD:

SPROUT SURPRISE SALAD

1. PEEL and SLICE the HARD-COOKED EGG. PUT one SLICE of EGG in the BOTTOM of an EMPTY PLASTIC YOGURT CUP.
2. PILE HALF of the alfalfa SPROUTS on the EGG.
3. PUT another SLICE of EGG on the SPROUTS.
4. PILE the REST of the alfalfa SPROUTS on THIS EGG.
5. LAY the CUCUMBER SLICE on the SPROUTS.
6. PUT the mayonnaise on TOP.
7. EAT YOUR SALAD as IS or WITH the mayonnaise mixed THROUGHOUT. THE TRICK IS TO EAT the SPROUTS and CUCUMBER and SAVE the EGG SURPRISE UNTIL the END.

Chapter 3

Out of the Giant Economy-size Trash Bag

Introduction

Making and eating too much of a favorite food and growing outlandishly large vegetables are the topics of the books in this chapter. Susan Heyboer O'Keefe's *One Hungry Monster* and David Wiesner's *June 29, 1999* are humorous in tone and appeal to children fascinated with great sizes and with stretching their imagination to the limits.

As funny as the images of "stuffed again" and the huge trash bag are, they suggest serious issues that the sensitive teacher or librarian will want to highlight. World hunger, recycling, and careful use of food resources are important for children to learn about and discuss. Even in our own country, food pantries, soup kitchens, and food purchased with food stamps remind us all that our food resources are limited for some.

The image of a trash bag for the chapter and for the starter kit may be unappealing, but it gives the teacher or librarian the perfect chance to talk about compost piles, throwing away as little food as possible, and recycling leftovers back to nature.

Children are fascinated by sizes of things in general, so large food and large quantities of food attract attention. Some children are "fussy" eaters or get locked onto one food and will eat nothing else. The books in this chapter help us all look at our personal eating patterns, laugh a little, and consider change.

Characters who eat lots of food include the frisky, hungry dog in *Hunky Dory Ate It* and all the little ants in *100 Hungry Ants*. Picky eater Nellie, in *No Peas for Nellie*, learns that all foods have value.

The focus book for this chapter, *June 29, 1999*, plays upon the concept of enormous food growing out of a third-grade science experiment. Reading about a child that can grow and launch gigantic vegetables will appeal to any kid who wants to have the ultimate science project and create an intergalactic sensation. The story stretches the limits of imagination and encourages the creation of other stories about giant vegetables landing on local doorsteps. The implications of giant food will provide the basis of more creative writing.

Science topics linked to this chapter include health and nutrition, ecology, and land use. Social studies issues such as world food distribution can be explored.

Focus Book

June 29, 1999, by David Wiesner, Clarion, 1992.

Holly has great expectations for her third-grade science project. She launches vegetable seedlings into the sky to study the effects of extraterrestrial conditions on vegetable growth and development. About one month later giant vegetables are discovered all over the United States. Holly becomes puzzled when the television news describes vegetable sightings that are not part of her experiment. She begins to wonder where these giant specimens came from and what happened to her vegetables. It seems they come from an extraterrestrial source, for the reader learns that a star cruiser from another galaxy accidentally jettisoned its vegetables into space about the same time Holly sent her vegetable seedlings into the sky.

Focus Book Activities

Written and Spoken Expression

Have students write and read news reports about the effects of the giant vegetables. Some could be straight news stories and others could be interviews with people from around the country who sighted the vegetables.

Written Expression

Make a list of other vegetables and other places where they could be sighted besides those that Wiesner describes in the book.

Written Expression

Choose one of the giant vegetable incidents to describe in greater detail. For example, Tony Kramer finds a giant cabbage on his farm in Ottumwa, Iowa, and declares that he will win a blue ribbon at the state fair. Create a story to tell about such an incident.

Spoken Expression

In this book two stories are happening at the same time. One is Holly's story about what happens to her vegetables, and the other story concerns the Acturian vegetables jettisoned from the star cruiser. Retell the two stories as two different readers theatre scripts of two plays.

Spoken Expression

Create a conversation between Holly and the captain of the Acturian spacecraft in the unlikely event that they would meet.

Written Expression

Holly will probably write up her science experiment in the form of a report. Write her report for her; include charts and pictures to show what she thinks happened.

Longer Read Aloud Book

Carris, Joan. *Just a Little Ham.* Illustrated by Dora Leder. Simon and Schuster, 1989. 135 pages.

Pandora likes junk food and riding in the car—but Pandora is a pig. Cary, Pandora's owner, has a hard time keeping Pandora's snooping snout out of the neighbors' gardens—and their lives.

Related Titles

Caplans, Peta. *Spaghetti for Suzy.* Houghton Mifflin, 1993.

Suzy likes lots of things, but most of all she likes spaghetti. Her parents think she'll either tire of it or turn into a noodle. When she shares her spaghetti with three animals, they help her discover that fruit also tastes good. But they all still enjoy spaghetti.

Demarest, Chris. *No Peas for Nellie.* Macmillan, 1988.

Nellie does not like peas, but she eats them. While she does, she lists all the other things she would rather eat: a python, a water buffalo (with salt and pepper, of course), and other exotic animals. When the list is complete the peas are gone. But now she has to finish drinking her milk!

Evans, Katie. *Hunky Dory Ate It.* Illustrated by Janet Morgan Stoeke. Dutton, 1992.

In rollicking rhymed lines, this is the story of Hunky Dory, a frisky, hungry puppy dog who eats everything. After devouring Clara Lake's cake and Sandy Deake's steak, the pup goes to the vet with a stomachache.

Gelman, Rita Golden. *More Spaghetti I Say.* Illustrated by Mort Gerberg. Scholastic, 1992.

Part of the "Hello Reading," beginning-reader series. The monkey in this rhymed text is too busy eating spaghetti to play with her friend Freddie.

Lent, Blair. *Molasses Flood.* Houghton Mifflin, 1992.

Based on an actual event, this fanciful recounting of the explosion of a molasses tank goes beyond the facts to tell of an entire city flooded with molasses. Luckily, the mess is cleaned up quickly, although everyone is tired of molasses before it is all eaten.

Mahy, Margaret. *Jam.* Illustrated by Helen Craig. Atlantic Monthly Press, 1985.

While Mr. Castle stays home and cares for the children (so Mrs. Castle can be an atomic scientist), the plum tree produces an abundance of ripe fruit. Mr. Castle makes so much plum jam that he ends up using it with eccentricity, such as stopping a leaky roof and repairing the floor. The family eats so much that they have terrible nightmares about jam. Just as they finish off the last jar in the pantry, the plum tree begins producing more ripe plums!

O'Keefe, Susan Heyboer. *One Hungry Monster.* Little Brown, 1992.

This rhymed counting book tells of hungry monsters searching the house for food. After they are fed they demand more food. Not until they are ordered outside does the boy who fed them bring out the apple muffin he was saving for himself.

Pinczes, Elinor. *100 Hungry Ants.* Illustrated by Bonnie Mackain. Houghton Mifflin, 1993.

In a single-file line of 100 hungry ants, one declares that they are traveling much too slowly to get to a picnic and that the food will likely be gone by the time they arrive. They decide to travel more efficiently—in two lines of 50, then in four lines of 25, then in five lines of 20, and finally ten lines of 10. When they arrive and the food is gone, 99 of the ants turn on the one who complained that they took too much time forming lines.

Slepian, Jan and Ann Seidler. *The Hungry Thing Goes to a Restaurant.* Illustrated by Elroy Freem. Scholastic, 1992.

The Hungry Thing has a problem with food names. He can't quite say them right and orders things like "bench flies with smetchup." Only children in the story, and children listening to the story, can figure out what he wants. Will he ever get full?

Wood, Don and Audrey Wood. *The Little Mouse, the Red Ripe Strawberry, and the Big Hungry Bear.* Child's Play, 1984.

Mouse tries all kinds of ways to hide his newly picked strawberry from Bear. The expressions on Mouse's face are comical as he disguises the strawberry with a fake nose, mustache, and glasses. Finally he finds the only way to keep the strawberry—eat it himself!

Ziefert, Harriet. *So Hungry.* Random House, 1987.

Kate and Lewis compete to make bigger and bigger sandwiches and eat them faster until they are no longer hungry.

Related Activities

Spice of Life

Tube Story

In a tube story, characters are mounted on cardboard rings and slipped onto a cardboard tube. The figures are flipped up and appear above the tube when the characters are in the action. For a small group of characters, use a paper-towel tube and rings made of 3-by-5-inch cards. Or make a huge tube out of the core from newsprint or photocopy paper.

For this story, make two tubes. The first one will have Peter; Peter, Jr.; Penny; and Paul. The second tube will have the mayor, Mama Antonio, and Mr. Beans.

The Price Spice Factory had been making spices and seasonings in Washingtown for over 100 years. The Price Spice Factory was a well-run operation. (Flip up Peter on tube one.) The president was Peter Price; his great grandfather had started the company. (Flip up Peter, Jr.) The vice president of sales was Peter Price, Jr., the son of Peter Price. (Flip up Paul.) The director of quality control was Paul Price, the younger brother of Peter, Jr. The advertising director was Penny Price, a sister to Peter, Jr., and Paul. (Flip up Penny.) Penny was the brightest member of the family.

Even though Price's Spices had been in business for a long time, the company was having a bad year. (Flip down all figures.)

In the spring, Penny Price had created a brand new advertising motto for the company. (Flip up Penny.) "Put a little spice in your life with Price's Spices—they are worth the price!" That improved sales a little, but not a lot. (Flip down Penny.)

By late summer sales had slumped drastically. (Flip up Peter, Jr.) "I've got a really hot idea for a sale. Let's slash the prices of our hottest spices. Let's sell chili powder and hot pepper seasoning for half the original price." But, not many people wanted hot spices in the summertime, so sales continued to drop. (Flip down Peter, Jr.)

(Flip up Peter.) By fall the company was in such bad shape that President Peter Price called a board meeting. (Flip up Peter, Jr. and Penny.) Peter, Jr., and Penny came right on time, but Paul was late.

(Flip up Paul.) He rushed into the room and announced, "An emergency! In all my years at Price Spice Factory nothing like this has ever happened."

"Simmer down, son," said President Peter.

"But, Dad, things are out of control."

"You are out of control. Simmer down and tell us all about it."

So Paul caught his breath and said, "I don't know how this happened, but for the last month we have only been making garlic salt."

There was a stunned silence and then President Peter said, "Only garlic salt?"

Paul nodded. "Only garlic salt."

(Flip down Peter, Jr., and Paul.) Peter, Jr., and Paul left the room and Penny said, "How dreadful. We must have variety. Variety is the spice of life."

"What can we do about this?" asked President Peter.

Penny said, "We have to store the stuff. Then I can come up with a plan." (Flip down all figures.)

So they filled all the vats and bins and crocks and cans, every container they found, with garlic salt. And Penny thought about a plan. She thought all through the fall and into the winter.

Winter came early that year—10 inches of snow the day before Thanksgiving. Snow and ice covered the streets all through December. By January the city was running out of salt to salt the city streets. Traffic was grinding to a halt. That's when Penny got a great idea.

(Flip up the mayor on tube two.) She called the mayor of Washingtown and made a deal with him. She would sell him all the garlic salt at half price. That way she could get rid of the salt and the city could keep on running.

The mayor said, "I'll take it!" And the street-salting trucks backed up to the Price Spice Factory and they were loaded with garlic salt. To everyone's relief, the garlic salt melted the ice on the streets. Soon traffic was flowing normally again. (Flip down the mayor.)

But that's not all that happened! The smell of the garlic salt made people hungry for pizza and spaghetti. (Flip up Mama Antonia.) Mama Antonia's Spaghetti House did a belly-popping business. "Mama mia—that garlic salt has saved my business! I've never sold so much spaghetti in all my life." (Flip down Mama.)

Since the people weren't sure where the garlic smell was coming from, each person thought, "It must be coming from me." (Flip up Mr. Beans.) So Mr. Beans of String-Beans Drugstore did big business in the areas of mouthwash and breath mints. "The sweet smell of success! All from the smell of garlic salt." (Flip down Mr. Beans.)

And, though no one knew for sure why, no vampires were sighted in Washingtown that winter.

Soon everyone in Washingtown felt that there were many benefits in having a lot of garlic around. (Flip up the mayor.) So the mayor called up President Peter and ordered enough garlic salt for the next winter. After all, the garlic salt did melt ice, and it was even cheaper than regular street salt. (Flip up Mama.) Mama Antonia ordered enough garlic salt to make spaghetti and pizza all year round. (Flip up Mr. Beans.) Then Mr. Beans from String-Beans Drugstore sent President Peter a letter of appreciation for keeping the city running. Sales of Price's Spices were soon mushrooming. (Flip down all figures.)

And in the spring, President Peter retired. The city honored the Price family with a special civic citation. (Flip up Penny.) The new president, Penny Price, received the award.

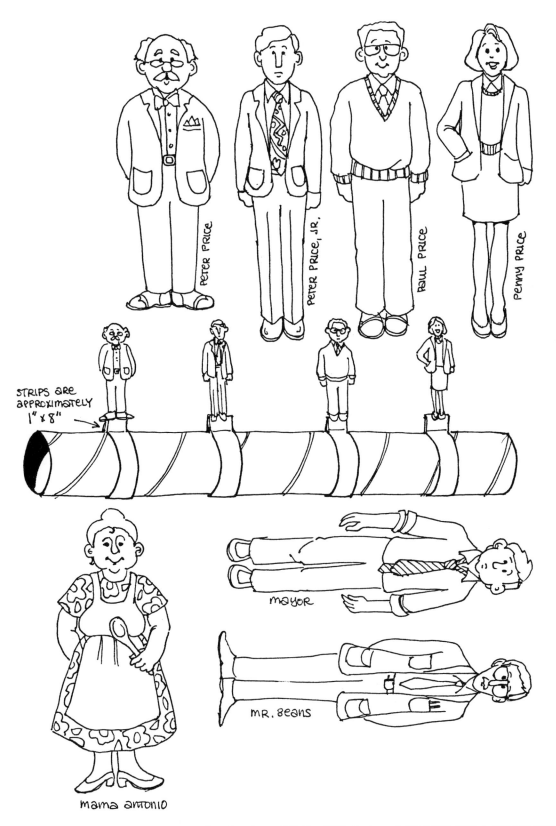

STRIPS are approximately 1" x 8"

PETER PRICE

PETER PRICE, JR.

PAUL PRICE

PENNY PRICE

mama antonio

mayor

mr. beans

Mashed Potato Mess

Characters:

Cousin Carrie
Grandma
Grandpa
Uncle Steve
Uncle Jake
Aunt Helen
Aunt Amy
Uncle Fred
Aunt Emily
Cousin Bob
Two Narrators

Stage setup: Arrange nine chairs or stools in a line or semicircle; a narrator stands at each end, and the relatives are seated with Cousin Carrie in the middle.

Readers theatre scripts are not meant to be memorized, but read with animation. After parts are assigned, let children read over the script to get a sense of the characters they will play. For the performance children can stand or be seated on stools. Occasionally, a character moves from one place to another (this is indicated in the script), but, in general, characters use body language to express emotions and action. For this script, characters face the audience when they talk on the phone and turn their backs to the audience when they are not interacting with Carrie. When the Thanksgiving guests start to arrive, characters turn to face the audience for the rest of the performance.

Narrator 1: Thanksgiving in the Howser family was steeped in tradition. They always went to Grandma's house where they had turkey and dressing.

Narrator 2: Whole cranberry sauce, corn ...

Narrator 1: Dinner rolls, relishes ...

Narrator 2: Pumpkin pie ...

Narrator 1: And plenty of mashed potatoes and gravy.

Narrator 2: But one year Grandma Howser decided she just couldn't face all that work.

Narrator 1: So Cousin Carrie offered to invite everyone to her condo.

Cousin Carrie: Hello, grandma? You and grandpa come to my place this year for Thanksgiving.

Grandma: I'll be happy to bring the turkey and dressing.

Cousin Carrie: That'll be just fine. But don't worry about the mashed potatoes because I've got them under control.... Hello, Aunt Helen? You and Uncle Steve can come to Thanksgiving at my condo this year.

Aunt Helen: I'll be glad to bring corn. I have some new recipes I want to try.

Cousin Carrie: That'll be just fine. But don't worry about the mashed potatoes because I've got them under control....Hello, Aunt Emily? I'm having Thanksgiving dinner at my condo this year. Can you come?

Aunt Emily: Of course! And I'll bring cranberry sauce with orange relish.

Cousin Carrie: That'll be just fine. But don't worry about the mashed potatoes because I've got them under control....Hello, Uncle Jake? I'm having Thanksgiving dinner at my condo this year. Can you come?

Uncle Jake: Sure. I'll bring the relish tray.

Cousin Carrie: That'll be just fine. But don't worry about the mashed potatoes because I've got them under control....Hello, Uncle Fred? I'm having Thanksgiving dinner at my condo this year. Can you and Aunt Amy come?

Uncle Fred: We'd love to, Carrie. Can we bring the pumpkin pies?

Cousin Carrie: That'll be just fine. But don't worry about the mashed potatoes because I've got them under control....Hello, Cousin Bob? I'm having Thanksgiving dinner at my condo this year. Can you come?

Cousin Bob: Sure. Let me bring the dinner rolls.

Narrator 2: As Thanksgiving Day drew closer, Carrie began to plan for the big meal. She looked at her pots and her pans.

Cousin Carrie: These will never do. I need bigger pots and pans and bowls to serve all those people. I wonder how much mashed potatoes I will need?

Narrator 1: Carrie went to the department store and bought ...

Cousin Carrie: A 10-quart cooking pot.

Narrator 2: And then Carrie went to the grocery store and bought ...

Cousin Carrie: 20 pounds of potatoes. I hope this is enough.

Narrator 1: Very early on Thanksgiving morning Carrie peeled ...

Cousin Carrie: Potatoes and potatoes and more potatoes. I certainly hope this is enough potatoes.

Narrator 2: Two hours later ...

Cousin Carrie: There. That does it for peeling 20 pounds of potatoes. I think I've got this under control.

Narrator 1: Carrie put those potatoes in the 10-quart pot and put it on the stove to boil. She set the table. The family started to arrive. First came Grandma and Grandpa.

Cousin Carrie: Grandma! How good to see you. Put the turkey right in the kitchen.

Grandma: I hope this 30-pound turkey will be plenty. I've got bread and corn bread stuffing, too. My, that certainly looks like a lot of potatoes you've got there.

Cousin Carrie: Sure is. I've got the mashed potatoes under control.

Narrator 2: Next came Aunt Helen and Uncle Steve.

Cousin Carrie: How nice you could come. What did you bring?

Aunt Helen: This is a new recipe for corn pudding.

Uncle Steve: And here is my favorite—creamed corn. Wow! Do you think you have enough potatoes?

Cousin Carrie: Sure do. I've got the mashed potatoes under control.

Narrator 1: Next came Aunt Emily and Uncle Jake.

Cousin Carrie: So good to see you. What have you got there?

Aunt Emily: I had to go to two stores to get enough cranberries for this crowd.

Uncle Jake: It took me three hours to peel these carrots. I bet it took you that long to peel all those potatoes.

Cousin Carrie: Quite a while, but I've got the mashed potatoes under control.

Narrator 2: The last time the doorbell rang it was Uncle Fred and Aunt Amy, with their pumpkin pies, and Cousin Bob.

Cousin Carrie: Welcome! Bring the pies into the kitchen. And Cousin Bob, those rolls smell wonderful.

Cousin Bob: I just baked them. Boy, did you make a lot of potatoes. Did Grandma forget the turkey or something?

Cousin Carrie: No, no. I have these mashed potatoes under control.

Narrator 1: Finally it was time to mash the potatoes.

Grandpa: Can I help you mash those potatoes?

Cousin Carrie: Sure. Would you like the old-fashioned potato masher or the mixer.

Grandpa: I'll try that fun-looking mixer.

Cousin Carrie: There sure are a lot of potatoes left in the pot. I'll put them in two big bowls. I wonder if I have another potato masher around here. Uncle Fred, would you give me a hand?

Uncle Fred: Sure! Hand me a masher.

Narrator 2: Grandpa mashed one pot's worth with the electric mixer.

Narrator 1: Uncle Fred mashed another pot of potatoes with an old-fashioned potato masher.

Narrator 2: And Carrie mashed a third pot of potatoes with another potato masher.

Cousin Carrie: I think we've got this under control.

Narrator 1: When the potatoes were mashed, Carrie piled hers into the big serving bowl. Then Uncle Fred loaded his on top of Carrie's.

Grandpa: Looks like that's plenty of mashed potatoes there, Carrie. I'll save mine for second helpings.

Narrator 2: That was a good idea ...

Narrator 1: Because when Carrie tried to pick up the serving bowl with all those mashed potatoes, she could hardly lift it.

Narrator 2: So Cousin Bob came to help.

Narrator 1: Together they heaved the bowl off the counter and staggered into the dining room.

Narrator 2: Two steps from the table, the bottom fell out of the bowl and the potatoes made a ...

Cousin Carrie: Mess! What a mess! These potatoes are completely out of control.

Grandma: There, there. No use crying over spilled potatoes. We'll clean them right up.

Cousin Carrie: But what's Thanksgiving without mashed potatoes? All we have is a mashed potato mess.

Grandpa: Now, Carrie. Here is another full pot of potatoes, enough for everyone to have a big helping.

Narrator 1: So the whole family gathered around the table and ate turkey and dressing, cranberries, corn, rolls, relishes, and pumpkin pie. And, of course, there was plenty of mashed potatoes.

Narrator 2: A new tradition was started in the Howser family. Cousin Carrie always brought the mashed potatoes because—after all, she had them under control.

Other Activities

Second Helpings Chant

This chant can be shared, as it is written here, with younger children. They can enjoy the rhythm and rhyme and add claps and actions along the way. The idea of a hungry tummy roaring and asking for more food appeals to younger children. Older children will add verses to create their own chants. The two lines "I'll eat so much/I just may pop" are used as a pattern. Show children that they can make this chant by thinking of a food for the first line of the stanza and, for the second line, another food to put on top of the first food. The words "on top" are also repeated. Thus a typical stanza might be: Mashed potatoes/gravy on top/I'll eat so much/I just may pop.

Food for my tummy
Hear it roar!
Food for my tummy!
Give me more!

Food for my tummy
Hear it roar!
Food for my tummy!
Give me more!

Mashed potatoes
Gravy on top
I'll eat so much
I just may pop!

Ice cream ice cream
Chocolate on top
I'll eat so much
I just may pop!

Food for my tummy
Hear it roar!
Food for my tummy!
Give me more!

Food for my tummy
Hear it roar!
Food for my tummy!
Give me more!

Whole wheat bread
Peanut butter on top
I'll eat so much
I just may pop!

Who Eats What?

Use the tune and format to the song "Bingo" to sing about greedy and picky eaters from the animal kingdom.

I knew a man who ate so much
He ate just like a hippo
H-I-P-P-O
H-I-P-P-O
H-I-P-P-O
He ate just like a hippo

I knew a man who hardly ate
He ate in little mouse bites
M-O-U-S-E
M-O-U-S-E
M-O-U-S-E
He ate in little mouse bites

Children can make up more stanzas for other animals with five-letter names. (Try horse, tiger, kitty, and rhino.)

Stanzas can be repeated, replacing one letter at a time in the spelled out word with a clap. For example, the second stanza of the hippo song would be:
I knew a man who ate so much

He ate just like a hippo
H-I-P-P-(clap)
H-I-P-P-(clap)
H-I-P-P-(clap)
He ate just like a hippo

Giant-Size Appetite

Imagine how much the giant in *Jack and the Beanstalk* had to eat to have enough energy to chase Jack! All the children can be giants with this chant. Teach them the giant's refrain and say it together.

Giant:

More food! More food!
More bread.
More meat.
Lots more to eat.
I want more!

Use a tray or platter and cut out pictures of food or plastic toy food. Begin with the leader's refrain.

Leader:

You want more food?
You want more food?
Here is more food.
How about ...?

Name a food you have and put it on the tray or platter. Children repeat the giant's refrain. Continue this dialogue until the platter is full. Then cover the platter and see how many of the foods the children can remember. Try having each child list them, and then combine all the lists. Leave the platter and food accessible so the children can play this game with each other.

Tempting Tall Tales

Some tall tales include food, such as Paul Bunyan's flapjacks. Have the class develop a "bigger than life" character, perhaps one who lives underwater or out in space. After the character has a name and attributes, have individuals or small groups decide what kind of food the character eats or cooks. How does too much of the food become a problem? How is the problem solved?

Another tall tale is an outright fantasy—just for fun and to stretch the imagination. Have children develop stories individually about themselves encountering too much or too little food. Where does it come from? How do they get rid of it? Or how do they get enough?

Or begin with a food, perhaps whatever the cafeteria is serving that day for lunch or some food that is available at a local fast-food restaurant. What would the class do if the hot dog cooker would not shut off?

Starter Kit

The "Out of the Giant Economy-size Trash Bag" Starter Kit will provide a visual aid that will introduce your food theme or unit quickly. No one can resist wondering what is inside a bag or basket, so just setting it on a display or holding it up will attract attention. The items inside the container will introduce the "flavor" of the food theme and start imaginations racing. In addition, many of the items will be used in specific activities or stories, so it is easy for you to assemble. It's all in the bag!

For this too-much-and-too-little food theme, you might pack these items into a large green trash bag. (Remember to recycle this bag to collect real garbage later.):

plastic animals to use with the song "Who Eats What?"
potato mashers and mixers and a copy of the script "Mashed Potato Mess"
assorted spices, especially garlic bulbs, to smell with the story "Spice of Life"
oriental cellophane noodles and popcorn to cook, and show how some foods can expand from a little to a lot
plastic food or cutout pictures for the activity "Giant-Size Appetite"
copy of the focus book *June 29, 1999*
assorted tall tales and myths that feature too much or too little food such as tales about Paul Bunyan
commercial-sized canned goods
foot-long hot dog
can of small Chinese corn
transparencies for "Who Eats What" and "Second Helpings Chant"
copies of the recipe pages for each child

Recipes

Melon Mess for a Mess of People

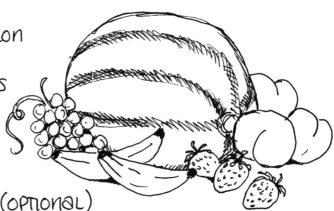

INGREDIENTS:

3 cantalopes or 1 watermelon
1 bunch of grapes
½-1 pound of strawberries
6 peaches
Lemon juice or fruit fresh
3 bananas
1 cup orange juice
½ cup shredded coconut (optional)

METHOD:

melon mess

1. FOR CANTALOPE: Cut a 2" slice from the top of the melon with a sharp knife and scoop out seeds and pulp with a spoon. Using a melon baller, scoop out cantalope balls and put them in a large bowl to mix with the rest of the fruit. Use these hollow cantalopes as containers.

2. FOR WATERMELON: Cut the melon in half, and using a melon baller or knife, hollow out some of one half of the melon. Use this hollow half as a container. From the removed melon make balls or chunks and put them in a large bowl to mix with the rest of the fruit. Either save the other half of the watermelon or cut it into balls or chunks to add to the fruit salad later, as the supply diminishes.

3. Wash all the fruits. Cut up the bananas. Hull the strawberries; leave them whole if they are small or slice them if they are large. Slice peaches, leaving on the skin if desired, and toss with lemon juice or fruit fresh so the peaches do not turn brown. Separate the grapes from the bunch. Add all this fruit to the large bowl with the melon.

4. Add orange juice and coconut to the fruit and mix. Spoon as much of the mixed fruit as you can into the melon containers. Keep the rest of the fruit in the bowl, covered, in the refrigerator, and replenish the melon containers as the crowd eats up the fruit!

Paul Bunyan-Sized Sandwich

INGREDIENTS:

2 FIVE-FOOT HOAGIE BUNS ORDERED from the BAKERY

MUSTARD in SQUEEZE BOTTLES

MAYONNAISE or SALAD DRESSING

WAXED PAPER

ANY INGREDIENTS the CHILDREN WANT ON THEIR SANDWICHES

(IF SCHOOLS or LIBRARIES ARE DOING THIS ACTIVITY, ASK EACH CHILD to BRING A FAVORITE INGREDIENT, SUCH AS LUNCH MEAT, CHEESE, or LETTUCE).

METHOD:

A PAUL BUNYAN-SIZED SANDWICH

1. COVER the SURFACE of A LARGE TABLE (6' LONG AT LEAST) WITH WAXED PAPER.
2. CUT the HOAGIE BUNS in HALF LENGTHWISE.
3. POSITION CHILDREN AROUND the TABLE. EACH CHILD HAS HIS or HER INGREDIENTS WITHIN REACH to PUT on the BREAD and to SHARE if THEY LIKE.
4. HAVE SOME CHILDREN AROUND the TABLE SPREAD the MAYONNAISE and MUSTARD on the BREAD.
5. PROVIDE PLASTIC KNIVES and SPOONS for SPREADING INGREDIENTS on the BREAD and INVITE ALL CHILDREN to HELP OUT.
6. HAVE AN ADULT HELP to COUNT CHILDREN and CUT the LOAVES into the APPROPRIATE NUMBER of PIECES. OLDER CHILDREN MAY LIKE to HELP WITH the CUTTING and SERVING.

Chapter 4

Out of the Doggie Bag

Introduction

Food is fun! In this chapter you can sample books about food you might only dream of eating, such as *Famous Seaweed Soup*. Cringe at the wicked surprises tucked in *Sam's Sandwich*. Stretch your imagination by creating funny food combinations, and think of foods like pickles that just sound fun. Some foods should never appear on the real dinner table. So just read *I Know an Old Lady Who Swallowed a Fly*. Sensitivity to cultural and even regional food preferences is essential. We can all learn to like new things!

In reality, food is only fun in a culture where there is already enough basic food to eat. We can only dream of imaginary food when our appetites are satisfied. Much of the world does not think of talking potatoes, but dreams of having real potatoes just to eat.

Because play is the natural realm for children, eating with humor is appealing. A baby with strained peaches knows what to do: rub them in her hair. The constraint of manners increases as children grow, and the desire to play increases. Babies can dump cereal on their heads and parents clean them up. If older children try this, it is not acceptable. But an older child can read a story about another child who does dump cereal and laugh at the results. Older kids like to carry this to the extreme by coming up with gross possibilities that children have to eat, such as fried worms or chocolate ants, which have been the topics of longer novels.

Any food can be funny, even the vegetable soup a dog eats in *Martha Speaks*. *Stop That Pickle* and *Sam's Sandwich* begin with an outlandish premise and only get funnier. The ultimate off-the-wall food book is *The Stinky Cheese Man*. Some books capitalize on the fun of food wordplay such as *Today Is Monday* and *Pass the Fritters, Critters*. One of the first silly food stories children hear is *I Know an Old Lady Who Swallowed a Fly*, which we include with several activities.

Old Black Fly, the focus book, is infectious fun, with wonderful rhyme, repeated refrain, and outlandish illustrations. Writing and speaking activities grow out of this book so naturally that we have included quite a few. More will come easily to the teacher or librarian who loves to have fun with food.

Focus Book

Old Black Fly by Jim Aylesworth. Illustrated by Stephen Gammell. Henry Holt,
    1992.

In this rollicking rhymed text a mischievous fly buzzes around the house causing
trouble from A to Z as he has a "very busy bad day."

Focus Book Activities

Spoken Expression

This text is so rhythmical it positively cries out to be read with syncopation. Help the
children discover the rhythm by having them slap legs or snap fingers as you speak the
words with primary stress. As an example, read the following two lines with stresses as
indicated: She áte on the crúst of the apple píe/He bothered the báby and máde her cry.
Shóo fly! Shóo fly! Shóoo.

Spoken Expression

After the text is read orally and syncopated as suggested above, have children create a
rhythm band to accompany their voice chorus. Make a full-scale oral presentation of this
book. Suggested instruments include wire whisks tapped in bowls, boxes of macaroni or
dried beans shaken and rattled, wooden spoons beaten on pans, spoons hit against each
other, and aluminum pie tins hit together. Divide the text into several parts and have
different groups of children read the lines. Have twenty-six readers participate, one for each
letter of the alphabet. Voices could be alternated to contrast deep and high vocal ranges.
Assign the "chorus" phrase "Shoo fly! Shoo fly! Shooo!" to everyone.

Written Expression

Write another prose story, parallel to this one, about the havoc the fly created; write
from another character's point of view. Some students may choose to write the story from
the perspective of the cat or the dog observing the day's events.

Written Expression

This story ends with the fly being swatted and splattered with the cake. Write another
ending with the fly escaping and then going to another house, a restaurant, or a supermarket
to begin his mischief all over again. The continuing story could have the fly "land on apples
and upset the cart, bump some bananas for just a start," and so on until he is finally swatted.
Try large or small groups of children. Try it as a cumulative rhyme with the first group
beginning the story then passing it on for another group to add to the verse. This may or
may not become an alphabet book. It may simply tell another fly story in rhyme.

Spoken and Written Expression

After the teacher reads the entire book, ask children to recall the trouble the fly caused.
Create a list of catastrophes the fly creates. Now make a new list of other things a fly might
do.

Spoken Expression with Bonus Art Activity

Much of the story is told through Gammell's expressive paintings. "Read" the pictures, as you read the words, by tracing the path of the fly with your finger. Have children retell the story by making a wordless book in the form of a long mural or banner. For the story banner, each child is given a panel of newsprint, 6 by 36 inches. The banner is folded into four panels so each child can draw four events from the story. Each child need not picture the same four events. This wordless retelling makes a good bulletin board and will encourage children to focus on story details.

Written Expression

This story is in the form of an alphabet book. Have students look for other alphabet books on a single theme and then write their own. The alphabet book might ask students to think of 26 actions centered around a single food, such as ate, baked, cut, diced, and so on, or 26 foods that a family shops for.

Spoken Expression

Discuss the total format and design of this book in relation to the text since both are intricately combined. Here are a few elements to keep in mind. Why did the illustrator choose to write the title in messy painted letters? If the title had been typeset in ornate script, what kind of fly might be the main character? A gourmet fly, for example. Note the use of black end pages and the use of a splatter trail of paint throughout the book and why these add to the overall story. How do the use of wild color and exaggerated details such as the large red eyes of the fly add to the growing frustration of the family?

Longer Read Aloud Book

Hodgman, Ann. *Stinky Stanley*. Illustrated by John Emil Cymerman. Simon and Schuster, 1993. 118 pages.

Lightning hits a loaded garbage can and—Phew!—out comes Stinky Stanley. He smells like a toxic waste dump and eats his own ear wax. Yuck!

Related Titles

Armour, Peter. *Stop That Pickle*. Illustrated by Andrew Shachat. Houghton Mifflin, 1993.

Various foods chase a pickle through city streets.

Carle, Eric. *Today Is Monday*. Philomel Books, 1993.

Each day of the week is matched with a special food and a funny animal to eat it. Beans stuck on a porcupine's quills and snakes wiggling in spaghetti make this traditional song a visual delight. Sunday is for ice cream and on Wednesday everyone can slurp "Zoooop"! The music is included.

Chapman, Cheryl. *Pass the Fritters, Critters*. Illustrated by Susan L. Roth. Four Winds, 1993.

Lots of animal names rhymed with food: "Pass the carrot, Parrot" and "Pass the honey, Bunny." But the animals will not share with a hungry boy. Even Mommy will not share her salami without the magic word "please." The illustrations are torn paper and torn napkins with cut-paper figures in bright colors.

Hale, Lucretia. *The Lady Who Put Salt in Her Coffee.* Illustrated by Amy Schwartz. Harcourt Brace Jovanovitch, 1989.

Written in 1867, this is the first of Hale's stories that were collected to become the "Peterkin Papers." The story unfolds as Mrs. Peterkin puts cream and a spoonful of salt in her coffee. A great many trials are made to remove it, some involving the local chemist and the herb woman. Finally the "Lady from Philadelphia," who helps with many of the Peterkins' dilemmas, suggests just pouring a new cup of coffee. The problem is solved!

Heller, Nicholas. *Peas.* Greenwillow, 1993.

After he refuses to eat his peas at supper, Lewis dreams they come alive and go for a wild ride on his electric train.

Howard, Jane. *When I Am Hungry.* Illustrated by Teri Sloat. Dutton, 1992.

A little boy acquires all kinds of animal characteristics, such as wings and the ability to breathe underwater, to experience all kinds of foods. The food he loves best is the supper on his own table.

I Know an Old Lady Who Swallowed a Fly. Illustrated by Glen Rounds. Holiday House, 1990.

Large, scraggy line drawings of animals and an old woman add to the humor of this favorite folk song about an old woman who swallows a bizarre feast.

Kasza, Keiko. *The Wolf's Chicken Stew.* Putnam, 1987.

A wolf who, more than anything in the world, loves to eat, develops a craving for chicken stew. Just as he prepares to grab a chicken for his prey, he decides to fatten her up. He cooks pancakes, donuts, and an enormous cake for the chicken and her brood. The chickens mistake all this as generosity. The wolf is so surprised by the results of doing something nice that he changes his intention.

Martin, Antoinette. *Famous Seaweed Soup.* Illustrated by Nadine Bernard Westcott. Whitman, 1993.

At the beach, a little girl wants to make seaweed soup. She gathers the water, seaweed, shells, sticks, and feathers all on her own because everyone in her family is busy. When the soup is done they all (pretend to) enjoy it.

Meddauth, Susan. *Martha Speaks.* Houghton Mifflin, 1992.

When Helen, a little girl, gives her dog, Martha, alphabet soup, the letters go to the dog's brain instead of her stomach. That evening the dog speaks. With a regular diet of alphabet soup, the dog converses with the startled family members and strangers. Problems begin when Martha talks too much. They stop feeding Martha alphabet soup, but then she cannot talk to save the family from a disaster. In the end they all learn a little moderation.

Numeroff, Laura. *If You Give a Mouse a Cookie.* Illustrated by Felicia Bond. HarperCollins, 1985.

If a hungry little mouse comes to visit, you might give him a cookie—but watch out. The mouse will want milk to go with it ... and on and on and on.

Numeroff, Laura. *If You Give a Moose a Muffin.* Illustrated by Felicia Bond. HarperCollins, 1991.

If a big hungry moose comes to visit and you give him a muffin to make him feel at home, the moose will want jam to go with it, and a whole lot more!

Pelham, David. *Sam's Sandwich*. Dutton, 1990.

Moveable flaps on pages open to reveal that bugs and slugs are included in the sandwich Sam makes for his sister. The bugs' names rhyme with text so the children can anticipate which bug is hiding in the sandwich.

Pelham, David. *Sam's Surprise*. Dutton, 1992.

Sam has rigged a box of lovely looking chocolates. Some of the "naughty" surprises inside the candies include a dead fish, pickled onion, toothpaste, and bubble gum. The book is shaped like a box of candy, with flaps and surprises on each page.

Pinkwater, Daniel. *Frankenbagel Monster*. Dutton, 1986.

Harold Frankenbagel is a popular baker, but his desire to be the greatest bagel maker drives him to invent Bageluculus. One night the monster goes wild and Frankenbagel must stop it. He does save the world: when Bageluculus goes stale outside a lox factory. But the world may not be safe from his next bagel invention.

Pinkwater, Daniel. *The Muffin Fiend*. Lothrop, Lee and Shepard, 1986.

Wolfgang Mozart helps the French police discover who is stealing all the muffins in Paris. It turns out to be an extraterrestrial creature who needs the muffins to fuel his trip home.

Sachar, Louis. *Monkey Soup*. Illustrated by Cat Bowman Smith. Knopf, 1992.

While Mommy prepares chicken soup to make Daddy feel better when he is sick in bed, the daughter makes her own soup for him with such fun items as bandages, a balloon, crayons, her blanket, buttons, and a stuffed monkey. Both soups make him feel better.

Scieszka, Jon. *The Stinky Cheese Man*. Illustrated by Lane Smith. Viking, 1992.

This collection of zany adaptations of fairy tales is funniest for those who are familiar with the original stories. Included are variants of Chicken Little, The Ugly Duckling, Little Red Riding Hood, and Jack and the Beanstalk. The wild illustrations add to the off-the-wall fun.

Wood, Audrey. *Heckedy Peg*. Illustrated by Don Wood. Harcourt Brace Jovanovitch, 1987.

A mother saves her children from a witch's spell that has changed them into different foods. She correctly guesses their true identities.

Related Activities

Going Bananas

An Object Story

As you tell this story, pass out bananas or large cutout banana shapes to the children playing the parts of the various characters. Mrs. McGillicutty puts her bananas in a flowerpot and then in a washtub and then she covers them with canned whipped cream or shaving cream to make a silly banana pie. Billy Bobby Brown tries to juggle his bananas. And the Morrises are given two monkey puppets. For a final touch, assemble a large banana split. Pass out a paper cup and a plastic spoon to each child so they can enjoy portions of this treat.

The Lightning Express rumbled through the town of Slipenslide at 12 o'clock noon. It was running behind, so Engineer Jed tried to pick up speed at the edge of town. Just as the train turned the bend to leave town, it derailed. No one was hurt, but carloads and carloads of bananas spilled all over the town. And that was the beginning of this crazy story that folks have told ever since.

Now everyone knows that bananas get ripe in a very short time, so even if the train could have been back on track right away, the bananas might have been too ripe by the time they were loaded back on the train. But the train couldn't get back on track to get to its next destination for at least three days.

Now that train did not just bump off the track in one slow easy bump. It bumped and it bumped and it bumped. Bananas went this way and that. Bananas landed everywhere.

B-U-M-P! The first train car bumped off the track.

Mrs. McGillicutty was in her kitchen when the first car derailed. One, two, three dozen bananas landed on her windowsill.

"Wow!" she exclaimed. "I love banana cream pie. With these bananas I'll make a banana cream pie, bigger than any I've ever made in my whole life."

So Mrs. McGillicutty made a huge pie crust, so huge it would not fit in her pie pan. She put the crust in a big flower pot. She filled the flower pot with the bananas, and she squeezed and shoved and pushed until the flower pot filled with banana cream pie fit in her refrigerator.

Across the street, Billy Bobby Brown was practicing magic tricks in his backyard when two of the biggest bananas he had ever seen suddenly appeared up in his apple tree.

"Whoa! My magic must really be working today!" he said. "I've pulled rabbits out of hats, but I've never turned apples into bananas. Right in the middle of my yard, too! With a little practice, bet I can learn to juggle."

So Billy Bobby picked up those bananas and started juggling. He started out tossing up just one banana, but before long he was tossing up both bananas and sometimes even catching them.

Over on the next block, the Morris family got the surprise of their lives when an armload of bananas fell down their chimney.

"Weird!" said Mrs. Morris.

"Wacky!" said Mr. Morris.

"Wonderful!" said Michael Morris. "I've always wanted a pet monkey. And now we have the perfect excuse."

The Morris family got in their car, drove to the pet shop, found a spirited little monkey, and took him to their house. The monkey felt right at home in a place that had so many bananas all ready and waiting.

B-U-M-P! The second train car bumped off the track.

One, two, three, four dozen more bananas landed on Mrs. McGillicutty's kitchen windowsill.

"Wow!" she exclaimed. "I love banana cream pie. With these bananas I'll make a second banana cream pie bigger than any I've ever made in my whole life."

So Mrs. McGillicutty made a huge pie crust, so huge it would not fit in her pie pan. She put that pie crust in a washtub. She filled the washtub with the bananas, and she squeezed and shoved and pushed until the washtub filled with banana cream pie fit in her refrigerator.

Across the street, two more giant bananas suddenly appeared in another apple tree in Billy Bobby Brown's yard.

"Whoa!" yelled Billy Bobby. "I must be the best magician and the best juggler in town." And Billy Bobby kept right on tossing up bananas and trying to catch them.

The Morris family was even more amazed when another armload of bananas fell down their chimney.

"Weird!" said Mrs. Morris.

"Wacky!" said Mr. Morris.

"Wonderful!" said Michael Morris. "I've always wanted a pet monkey. And now we have the perfect excuse."

The Morris family got back in their car, drove to the pet shop, found another little monkey, and took him to their house. The monkey felt right at home in a place that already had a monkey and so many bananas all ready and waiting.

B-U-M-P! B-U-M-P! B-U-M-P! Three more train cars bumped off the track.

One, two, three, four, five, six, seven, eight, nine, ten, eleven, twelve dozen more bananas landed on Mrs. McGillicutty's kitchen windowsill.

"Whew!" said Mrs. McGillicutty. "I love banana cream pie, but this is too much. I am going bananas!"

Two, four, six, eight, ten more bananas suddenly appeared in Billy Bobby's apple tree.

"Whoa!" said Billy Bobby. "I must be the best magician in the whole world, but I am not the best juggler. I am going bananas!"

Well, Mr. and Mrs. Morris were shocked speechless when a truckload of bananas fell down their chimney.

"Wonderful! Wonderful! Wonderful!" shouted Michael Morris. "Now I can have a house full of monkeys!"

"No," said Mr. Morris. "No more monkeys."

"I would go bananas," said Mrs. Morris.

And indeed the whole town seemed to be going bananas. Bananas landed in the town square, bananas fell in the park, and bananas filled the streets.

"What will we do?" cried Mrs. McGillicutty. "I don't have a big enough washtub to make any more pies. I am going bananas."

"I can't juggle any more bananas!" shouted Billy Bobby Brown. "I am going bananas!"

"We don't have any more room for any more monkeys!" screamed Mr. and Mrs. Morris. "We are going bananas!"

"Wonderful!" said Michael Morris, "Let's all go bananas. I have a great idea."

Michael called up the Street Department and trucks with scoops and fork lifts came and cleaned up all those bananas.

Michael called up the Parks and Recreation Department and they drained all the water from the town swimming pool. The trucks filled the pool with all those bananas, and everyone agreed to help peel them.

The town dairy delivered enough ice cream and whipped cream to cover all those bananas. And before you could say "going bananas," the world's biggest banana split was assembled in the town pool.

Now, no one knows if this story is true. They say there was enough food for a month of sundaes. It sounds crazy. But that's what folks say when they tell about the time the whole town of Slipenslide went bananas.

Ebeneezer in the Freezer

Characters:

David
Jenny
Mother
Father
Four Narrators

Stage setup: Arrange eight chairs or stools in a line or semicircle; seat narrators at the ends.

Readers theatre scripts are not meant to be memorized, but read with animation. After parts are assigned, let children read over the script to get a sense of the characters they will play. For the performance, children can stand or be seated on stools. Occasionally, a character moves from one place to another (this is indicated in the script), but, in general, characters use body language to express emotions and action. For this script, place a toy frog—Ebeneezer—in a clear plastic box.

Narrator 1: We'd like to tell you the silly tale of an underwater toad—

Narrator 2: Or what used to be an underwater toad—

Narrator 1: By the name of—

Narrator 2: Ebeneezer.

Narrators 3 and 4: Ebeneezer in the freezer, Ebeneezer in the freezer.

Narrator 1: He didn't start out that way.

Narrator 2: No, he didn't. Let's go back to the beginning of the story.

Narrator 1: Once upon a time ...

Narrator 2: Not THAT long ago.

Narrator 1: All right. Two years ago, David Oliver asked for a turtle for his birthday.

Narrator 2: But the pet store owner told David's mother that turtles weren't sold as pets anymore so she'd have to choose something else.

Narrator 1: That something else was a ...

David: A TOAD! I didn't ask for a toad.

Mother: I know you didn't, but this is the closest thing I could find. It's an underwater toad. It can live all summer in this fish tank. We just have to keep the top covered so he doesn't jump out.

David: He looks lively all right.

Mother: What will you name him?

David: Hmmm. It will have to be something special. I don't like just any old name for an underwater toad. I don't know anyone who has an underwater toad. Let's see ... Tommy? Warty? Naw. Mom, do you think it's a boy toad?

Mother: I really don't know, David.

David: I'll bet he is. He looks just like this geezer I saw downtown last week. Geezer! Hey! I've got it! I'll call him "Ebeneezer!"

Narrator 1: So that's how Ebeneezer got his name.

Narrators 3 and 4: Ebeneezer in the freezer, Ebeneezer in the freezer. In the freezer—there's Ebeneezer!

Narrator 1: Let's get on with the story.

Narrator 2: David loved Ebeneezer.

David: Eb, you are just about the best thing that ever happened to me. You always make me feel better. I can tell you all my secrets. And you never talk back to me.

Narrator 1: David didn't have a lot of friends.

David: Ebeneezer, you are my best friend.

Narrator 2: All summer long David watched Ebeneezer jump. David fed him two small pinches of toad food every day. He moved the fish tank every other day so Ebeneezer could have different views of the room. And David carefully changed Ebeneezer's water to keep him healthy.

Narrator 1: But, for some reason, Ebeneezer died the day before school was to start.

Mother: David, I'm really sorry. I know how much you loved Ebeneezer.

Father: Maybe you'd feel better if you had a funeral for him.

Mother: I think that's an excellent idea.

Narrator 2: So David put Ebeneezer in the plastic box that held his watch.

Narrator 1: And he buried Ebeneezer in the back yard.

Narrator 2: For one night.

David: Oh, Ebeneezer, I miss you. You must be lonely out there in the back yard.

Narrator 1: So he dug up Ebeneezer.

David: (Holding plastic box) Now what can I do with you?

Narrator 2: Jenny, David's younger sister, saw David holding Ebeneezer's box.

Jenny: Mama, David dug up his old toad.

David: Jenny, you're a stinking rotten tattletale!

Jenny: I stink? He stinks!

David: He does not stink.

Jenny: Well, he will if you keep him out very long. It's still summer, you know.

David: For your information, I'm going to put him on ice so he'll be frozen and preserved forever.

Jenny: Dad, David is putting Ebeneezer in the freezer.

Father: Well, just be sure you label the container. We certainly don't want to eat him by mistake.

David: Dad, how could you say such a thing?

Jenny: Yuck! I'm not eating anything in this house for a month!

Narrator 1: The next day, Mother sent Jenny down to the freezer for a package of hamburger to make spaghetti.

Jenny: Mom, you're all out of hamburger.

Mother: All right. I'll look. (Looking in freezer) Chicken. Shrimp. Here's the hamburger and what (pulling out the box) is this? It looks like it says "Ebeneezer."

Narrators 3 and 4: Ebeneezer in the freezer, Ebeneezer in the freezer. In the freezer—there's Ebeneezer!

David: Mom, could you let him rest in peace?

Mother: David, I do wish you'd bury that toad out in the yard.

Narrator 1: But David put Ebeneezer back in the freezer.

Narrator 2: The next day, Mother sent Jenny down to the freezer for a package of chicken to make enchiladas.

Jenny: Mom, there isn't any chicken down here.

Mother: Oh, yes there is. I saw it yesterday.

Jenny: I can't find it.

Mother: Oh, all right. I'm coming. (Looking in freezer) Shrimp. Here's the chicken. And what is this? Oh, no. It's Ebeneezer.

Narrators 3 and 4: Ebeneezer in the freezer, Ebeneezer in the freezer. In the freezer—there's Ebeneezer!

Mother: David! What did I ask you to do?

David: I know, Mom, but I just wanted to keep him one more day.

Narrator 1: But the next day came ...

Narrator 2: And Mother sent Jenny down to the freezer for the shrimp.

Jenny: Mom, we don't have any shrimp down here.

Mother: Jenny, please look again.

Jenny: Mom, all I found was ...

Mother: Don't tell me.

Jenny: Ebeneezer.

Narrators 3 and 4: Ebeneezer in the freezer, Ebeneezer in the freezer. In the freezer—there's Ebeneezer!

Mother: David, you've got just one more chance.

David: Mom, just one more day.

Mother: All right. I'm coming to get that shrimp. And David, I'm giving you one more day to bury that toad.

Narrator 1: The next day, Mother sent Jenny down to see if there was anything left in the freezer to cook for dinner.

Jenny: Mom, you'd better come down here right away.

Mother: What's wrong? Has the freezer quit running?

Jenny: No, Mom. The freezer is empty.

Mother: Then we'll just have to go to the store.

Jenny: But Mom, what happened to ...

Mother: Ebeneezer!

Jenny: Mom, you didn't cook him last night did you. That shrimp jambalaya sure looked different!

Mother: David, where is Ebeneezer?

David: Ebeneezer is resting in peace.

Mother: Then you buried him?

David: Yes, Mom.

Mother: Good. I'm relieved.

Father: I'm glad, son. Say, what are we having for dinner? I'm hungry as a bear.

Mother: Sorry, I need to go to the store. What would you like for dinner?

Jenny: Chinese.

Father: That does sound good. And now that Ebeneezer's not in the freezer, we don't have to worry about Mom mixing him up in the stir fry!

David: Dad, how could you say such a thing.

Mother: Oh, David, Ebeneezer was a good toad. But I'm glad he's not in the freezer.

Narrators 3 and 4: Ebeneezer in the freezer? No Ebeneezer in the freezer—not around. Not around? Ebeneezer's in the ground.

Narrator 1: And that's the end—

Narrator 2: Of our silly, silly tale.

Other Activities

I Know an Old Lady: A Silly Song to Make Up

Writing Activity

The favorite folk song *I Know an Old Lady Who Swallowed a Fly* can be a springboard for classroom writing activities. Here are several ways to begin.

Give each child a large sheet of paper headed with the line: "I know an old lady who swallowed a _____." Suggest that they think of a word to complete the sentence that can be rhymed in this manner: "I know an old lady who swallowed a fly./I don't know why she swallowed a fly." For example, a student might write, "I know an old lady who swallowed a frog./She sat on a log to catch a frog." After the verse is written, the student draws a picture of the episode.

After all students create their song verses, papers are gathered. Students read and share them. Perhaps the pictures can be displayed while other students guess the lines or suggest alternative lines. Sing the verses one after another.

The class may create a silly song in cumulative sequence. This could be done in small groups. Each group begins with a different small animal in the first rhymed verse and creates a series of rhymed verses in which the old lady eats larger and larger animals until she pops. An example of a sequence of small animals with rhymed possibilities might be: gnat/that, frog/log, snake/mistake, owl/scowl, bobcat/that, bear/care. The ending verse could be: "And then she popped./Our song has stopped."

Mucked-up Menus

Writing Activity

Because kids, especially those in middle grades, relish slightly gross humor, the song "Great Green Gobs of Greasy Grimy Gopher Guts" has long enjoyed popularity. Incorporate this appeal into a writing activity. Students will be inspired to think imaginatively and build their vocabulary.

Before you begin, discuss the idea of eating unusual foods. What seems unusual to some may be usual for others. For example, in some parts of the United States, people eat pigs' feet; this may seem strange to some students. In China, pigs' ears are eaten. Snails are a delicacy in France, and haggis (a mixture of meats and oatmeal boiled in an animal stomach) is cooked in Scotland.

Students will enjoy creating their own mucked-up menus and these menus can still be sensitive to food preferences around the world if the teacher provides specific examples such as those above. Think of odd combinations of usual foods, such as mashed potatoes served with marshmallows. Think of cooking and eating things of ridiculous size. Eating a gnat seems silly given its nearly microscopic size, for example. Imagine cooking and eating something that does not really exist in a tangible form such as cooking a pig's squeal or eating a dog's bark. Combine these ideas with cooking methods such as boiling, baking, frying, and stir frying, and with seasonings such as curry powder, pepper, and paprika.

Brainstorm with students to create a long list of far-out food combinations. Then invite students to design mucked-up menus for a ridiculous restaurant.

A starter menu
Marshmallow Mashed Potatoes
Peanut-Butter-and-Liver Sandwiches
Ice Cream Sundae Topped with Tomato Sauce
Steak Garnished with Gnats
Pizza with Sauerkraut and Pickles
Pig's Squeal Baked in a Pie
Creamed Newt Brains on Toast
Boiled Hippopotamus Tongue
Curried Cricket Feet
Stir-Fried Bat Wings
Night Crawler Soup

Smart-Cookie Food Riddles

Kids will be able to make up their own food riddles and jokes with just a little coaxing. The teacher or librarian can begin by asking kids to think of common food expressions such as "in a pickle," and "going bananas." Students may wish to consult a dictionary of idioms or clichés and add those about food to their stock of expressions. Then ask kids to draw pictures of their food riddles.

Picture riddles have been around for several hundred years. In the early days of television, the humorist Roger Price coined the phrase "droodles" to describe a drawing and a doodle combined. Price's droodles presented an odd view of an object. Kids will be fascinated by this idea.

The food picture riddles below are a little less distorted. Some of the picture riddles are visualizations of food clichés, and others are odd explanations for the pictures. Notice that several answers are possible for some of the following.

Not my cup of tea
In a pickle
A finger in every pie
Apple of her eye
A pan of brownies cut out by a kid who doesn't like edges
An offbeat donut with a square hole or a pat of butter on a stack of pancakes (cousins to a square peg in a round hole)

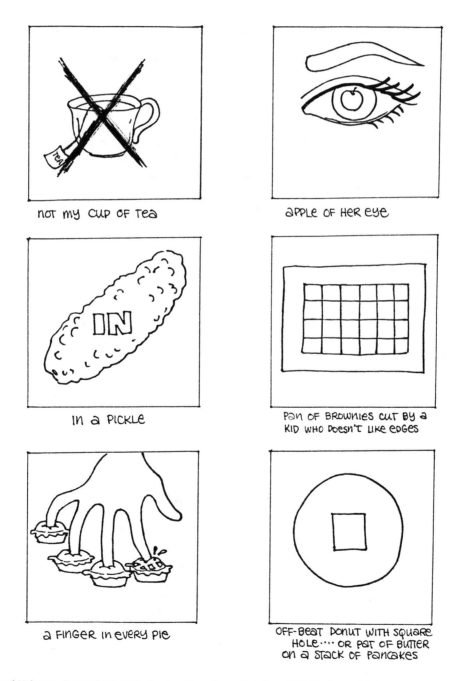

not my cup of tea

apple of her eye

in a pickle

pan of brownies cut by a
kid who doesn't like edges

a finger in every pie

off-beat donut with square
hole···· or pat of butter
on a stack of pancakes

Playing with Your Food

Even kids who think they do not like creative writing enjoy the fast action and snappy dialogue of comic strips.

On a sheet of paper, 9 by 18 inches, draw four equal-sized rectangles. These will be the frames for a cartoon story starring an edible super hero each child will invent, such as "Aunt Asparagus," or "The Zucchini Zoomer." A four-frame story needs a beginning, a middle, and an end. Punctuation and spelling are still important, and neatness counts when you are putting words and pictures into one box.

After completing these adventures, shrink these comic strips on a photocopy machine that reduces pictures and put them in a newsletter or compile them in a scrap book.

Someday Wonder Watermelon may be a reality!

The Yoke's On You

One reason food is so much fun to think and talk about is that the names of food (or words that sound like them) frequently turn up as other parts of speech. For example, "if you break an egg the YOKE's on you," and "you wouldn't have dropped it if he hadn't EGGED you on." Some of the phrases adults find funny may at first be lost on children who do not have the background to get the joke. However, language today has taken on meanings that adults may not be aware of, so they may need to have some jokes explained to them!

To start a joke-and-riddle writing session, make a list of food words that have homonyms. Then make another list of food words and common words that rhyme. Finally generate a list of food words and names that are just fun to say.

In small groups the children can work with these lists of words to make their own jokes. (Remember, "corny" is a high compliment for a food joke!)

Name That Tune

These songs will never be in the top 20 (but, who knows? "Yes, We Have No Bananas" may have started as a classroom activity!), but they will expand vocabularies and incite some silly-food fun.

Choose a tune that is easy for you to sing, perhaps a nursery rhyme or a camp song. Then brainstorm lists of different foods that all begin with the same letter. Now have pairs of children choose a letter and use the tune to write a song that incorporates as many of the food words as possible. For example, if the tune is the chorus to "Mine Eyes Have Seen the Glory," a song about the letter "b" might be:

I like bunches of banana
Bread and jam of boysenberry
Brussels sprouts and beef chop suey
And that's my song about "b"!

For more action, have the pairs of writers sing their songs. The rest of the children must alternately stand up and sit down each time they hear the featured letter.

P-I-Z-Z-A

(To the tune of "Bingo")

I had a pizza all my own
And all of it was mine-o.
P-I-Z-Z-A,
P-I-Z-Z-A,
P-I-Z-Z-A,
And all of it was mine-o!

I had a pizza that I shared
One piece went to my brother.
P-I-Z-Z-(clap),
P-I-Z-Z-(clap),
P-I-Z-Z-(clap)
But all the rest was mine-o!

I had a pizza that I shared
One piece went to my sister.
P-I-Z-(clap, clap),
P-I-Z-(clap, clap),
P-I-Z-(clap, clap),
But all the rest was mine-o!

I had a pizza that I shared
One piece went to my mother.
P-I-(clap, clap, clap),
P-I-(clap, clap, clap),
P-I-(clap, clap, clap),
But all the rest was mine-o!

I had a pizza that I shared
One piece went to my father.
P-(clap, clap, clap, clap),
P-(clap, clap, clap, clap),
P-(clap, clap, clap, clap),
But all the rest was mine-o!

I had a pizza that I shared
One piece is all I'm left-o.
(clap, clap, clap, clap, clap),
(clap, clap, clap, clap, clap),
(clap, clap, clap, clap, clap),
And now that piece is gone-o!

Starter Kit

The "Out of the Doggie Bag" Starter Kit will provide a visual aid that will introduce your food theme or unit quickly. No one can resist wondering what is inside a bag or basket, so just setting it on a display or holding it up will attract attention. The items inside the container will introduce the "flavor" of the food theme and start imaginations racing. In addition, many of the items will be used in specific activities or stories, so it is easy for you to assemble. It's all in the bag!

For this silly-food theme, you might pack these items in a restaurant doggie bag:

an ice cube with a plastic frog frozen in it and a copy of the script "Ebeneezer in the Freezer"
cards with food jokes on them
copy of the focus book *Old Black Fly*
puppet of the "Old Lady" who swallowed a fly
copy of *Sam's Sandwich* or *Sam's Surprise*
plastic toy food of all kinds
assorted plastic insects and objects
gummy worms, for a treat
silly cereal and silly pasta in plastic bags, such as dinosaur-shaped cereal
people crackers for your dog

lots of bananas for the story "Going Bananas"
jar of pickles
transparency of the song "P-I-Z-Z-A"
paper and pencils for the writing activities

Recipes

Silly Spaghetti Soup

Ask kids what foods are silly and someone is certain to answer "spaghetti." Why? Because it wiggles and because it makes you giggle when you try to wrap it around your fork and eat it. Build on these ideas by creating a silly food combination for this recipe.

The idea of spaghetti soup is silly, but the method for making it is smart. Cooks know it is not easy to estimate how much spaghetti to cook for a crowd, or even just one person. A spaghetti-hole measure can be drawn the size of a quarter on index cards for children to take home and use. Simply stick a small handful of thin spaghetti through the hole to determine how much will be enough for this recipe.

INGREDIENTS:

(FOR ONE SERVING OF SOUP)
1 10 3/4 ounce can of condensed tomato soup
1 soup can of water to prepare the soup
1 cup of cooked spaghetti
4 cups of water to boil the spaghetti
1 tablespoon of grated parmesan cheese

METHOD:

SILLY SPAGHETTI SOUP

1. EMPTY TOMATO SOUP from the can into a pan or bowl and add 1 soup can of water to dilute the soup. STIR THIS WELL, UNTIL THERE ARE NO LUMPS in the SOUP. POUR 1 CUP OF THIS TOMATO SOUP mixture into an INDIVIDUAL SOUP BOWL.
2. TAKE a SMALL HANDFUL of the SPAGHETTI and STICK IT THROUGH the SPAGHETTI-HOLE measure to DETERMINE HOW MUCH to COOK.
3. MEASURE the 4 CUPS of WATER into a PAN or POT and HEAT UNTIL the WATER IS BOILING. ADD the SPAGHETTI and BOIL IT for 5 minutes.
4. DRAIN the WATER from the SPAGHETTI USING a COLANDER.
5. STIR the SPAGHETTI into the SOUP BOWL.
6. SPRINKLE the CHEESE on the TOP.
7. COVER the SILLY SPAGHETTI SOUP with PLASTIC WRAP and COOK in the MICROWAVE at HIGH POWER for 2 minutes.
8. EAT. WITH a FORK and a SPOON! HOW SILLY!

Going Bananas Recipes

(For Bananas That Are Almost Rotten!)

What do you do when bananas start to rot? Don't go bananas and throw them away. Just mash them up and use them in one of the following recipes. You can also use them, mashed or chopped, in the frozen ice cream cups on this page.

Funny Fruit Freeze

INGREDIENTS:

1 CUP CRUSHED PINEAPPLE
2 SOFT BANANAS
1/4 CUP ORANGE JUICE
1 PACKAGE FROZEN STRAWBERRIES, SLIGHTLY THAWED

METHOD:

FUNNY FRUIT FREEZE

1. IN A BOWL, MASH UP THE PEELED BANANAS WITH A FORK. ADD PINEAPPLE, SLIGHTLY THAWED STRAWBERRIES, and ORANGE JUICE.
2. SPOON into PAPER BAKING CUPS in 12-MUFFIN TINS. COVER WITH FOIL.
3. FREEZE for 4 to 5 HOURS.
4. SERVE FROZEN.

Banana Milk Shake

INGREDIENTS:
1 CUP ICE CREAM
1 SOFT BANANA
½ CUP MILK

METHOD:

BANANA MILK SHAKE

1. IN A MIXING BOWL, MASH UP PEELED BANANA WITH A FORK. ADD SLIGHTLY SOFTENED ICE-CREAM AND MILK.
2. MIX WITH AN ELECTRIC HAND MIXER OR IN A BLENDER. POUR INTO A GLASS.

Banana Surprise Muffins

INGREDIENTS:
¼ CUP MILK
1 EGG
MUFFIN MIX
1 SOFT BANANA

METHOD:

BANANA SURPRISE MUFFINS

MAKE MUFFINS ACCORDING TO PACKAGE DIRECTIONS, ADDING ONE MASHED BANANA TO THE RAW MIX!

Chapter 5

Out of the Carry-Out Box

Introduction

Restaurant dining has become a standard experience in our culture. We have more discretionary income and less time to cook. For many children, eating out and picking up carry-out food are parts of their weekly routine. Drive-ins have evolved into drive-up windows. Even the grocery store provides carry-out food—in the deli department, and in the frozen-food aisle. All this is a commentary on the fast-paced lifestyle where the microwave is the family mealtime center.

Having company for dinner used to mean ironing the white tablecloth, polishing the silver, and filling the nut cups. Now it can include a backyard barbecue or sharing a pizza. The idea is the same: Eat with people you do not normally eat with and share food and experiences. Traditionally, this includes the Sunday dinner, potluck suppers, and pancake and chili suppers. There has been a rebirth of special-occasion events such as tea parties.

Both eating out and picking up carry-out food engage kids. Restaurants have prepackaged meals marketed for a child's appetite, and frozen-food companies package entrees with a child's tastes in mind. Children can relax in these atmospheres and learn skills such as decision making and ordering.

Karen Barbour's *Little Nino's Pizzeria* and Nancy Shaw's *Sheep Out to Eat* will remind children of the fun of eating out. And when company is coming, think of the fun if they bring food to share for some dinner time surprises.

Chicken Sunday, the focus book for this chapter, is much more than a food book. It is a story about family relationships, ethnic understandings and misunderstandings, the resourcefulness of children, and special bonds between people. The food focus is the Sunday dinner at Miss Eula Mae's; the children enjoy fried chicken with all the trimmings. Miss Eula Mae associates the sharing of chicken with the sharing of love, so closely that she asks the children to pour chicken broth over her grave so she will have it always. The children keep their promise.

Follow a reading of this book with art projects—researching the folk art in *Chicken Sunday*, making collages that include family photographs, and designing Pysanky eggs. Other curricular activities growing out of this chapter include writing, in different formats. Children design their own menus, write food ads, and create jokes and riddles for sample restaurant placemats.

Focus Book

Chicken Sunday, by Patricia Polacco. Philomel, 1992.

Three children want to buy Miss Eula Mae Walker a special hat for Easter, to thank her for her special Sunday chicken dinners, but they do not have enough money. One day, they are mistakenly accused of throwing eggs at Mr. Kodinski's hat shop, and they come up with a plan to make amends. They make beautifully decorated Pysanky eggs that he agrees to sell in his shop. Then he gives the children the prized hat and they give it to Miss Eula Mae. The old woman tells them she can die happy now, but she makes them promise that when she is dead they must boil up a chicken and pour the broth over her grave so she will have chicken always.

Focus Book Activities

Spoken Expression

Role play the different episodes in this story. One episode could be the children trying to explain to Miss Eula Mae that they did not throw the eggs. Another episode could be the children taking their eggs to Mr. Kodinski's shop.

Spoken Expression

Discuss the design elements of this book that add to its visual appeal, such as the purple endpapers that remind the reader of the Easter season, the use of line, the collage photographs of the family, and the richly designed Pysanky eggs.

Curricular Connection

Have students research the folk art shown in the book and learn more about Russian and Polish design.

Written Expression

Miss Eula Mae is a strong female character in this story. Have children write her life story or describe her in greater detail.

Written Expression

The Sunday dinners at Miss Eula Mae's will remind children of special family meals they have enjoyed or experienced. Have children write about a meal they remember or have them interview a family member about a holiday meal shared with people who were like family.

Spoken Expression

The children are unjustly accused of throwing eggs at Mr. Kodinski's hat shop. Have children tell about a time they got blamed for trouble they did not cause.

Written and Spoken Expression

Have children brainstorm a list of ways they might raise money to buy something special for a person they love.

Written Expression

Polacco's expression "a voice that sounded like slow thunder and sweet rain" is especially memorable. Have children create expressions to describe other voices such as "a voice that sounded like sunshine and warm summer nights."

Longer Read Aloud Book

Paterson, John. *The Littles Give a Party.* Illustrated by Roberta Carter Clark. Scholastic, 1972. 96 pages.

The Bigg family does not know that there is another family living in their house: Meet the Littles. They eat leftovers and use items the family no longer needs for amazing inventions. In this adventure, Grandma Little's surprise birthday party has the Littles scrambling for picnic fare.

Related Titles

Barbour, Karen. *Little Nino's Pizzeria.* Harcourt Brace Jovanovitch, 1987.

Tony enjoys helping his dad operate Little Nino's, a successful, small pizza restaurant. But when the father opens a fancy, expensive restaurant, no one has fun. In the end, changing back to the smaller restaurant restores the family's pride and enjoyment.

Cuyler, Margery. *Daisy's Crazy Thanksgiving.* Illustrated by Robin Kramer. Henry Holt, 1990.

Daisy's family operates Rockwell's cafe. Daisy likes to help with the dishes, but holidays are a nightmare. One Thanksgiving, thinking she can get away from the crazy business at the cafe, Daisy visits Grandma ... and Aunt Millie's dog, cats, and monkey; a food-throwing baby; and a turkey that never thaws. She decides it is actually less crazy at home.

Dalmais, Anne Marie. *The Busy Day of Mamma Pizza.* Illustrated by Graham Percy. Farrar, Straus & Giroux, 1990.

Mamma Pizza, a kindhearted elephant, operates a bustling Italian restaurant with an assortment of animal customers that ranges from an elegant donkey to a difficult wild boar. She works hard all day to keep the customers happy and well-fed with her famous spaghetti.

Dragonwagon, Crescent. *Alligator Arrived with Apples: A Potluck Alphabet Feast.* Illustrated by Jose Aruego and Ariane Dewey. Macmillan, 1987.

The first to arrive is Alligator with apples. This alphabet book celebrates animals and food. The last to arrive is Zebra with zucchini. Then all the guests gather for a Thanksgiving feast.

Falwell, Cathryn. *Feast for 10.* Clarion, 1993.

A mother and five children shop with one shopping cart for two pumpkin pies, five kinds of beans, and other numbers of items. At home they repeat the counting when preparing the meal, setting eight platters on the table, and inviting friends to have 10 people eating. The illustrations are cut-paper figures with interesting textures and bright colors.

Field, Rachael. *General Store*. Illustrated by Nancy Winslow Parker. Greenwillow, 1988.

Rachel Field's 1926 poem details all the fun things in a general store: such as peppermints, bananas, and sarsaparilla. The colored-pencil drawings of a little girl dreaming of this store enliven the poem.

Greenberg, Melaine. *My Father's Luncheonette*. Dutton Books, 1991.

A little girl is her father's best customer at his dinette. She orders from the menu, sits on a revolving stool, and she helps with child-size jobs such as bringing the waitress a glass of water. At last she and her father turn off the lights, lock up, and go home. The pictures are done in bold colors that set off the wonderful black-and-white tile floor in the luncheonette.

Koller, Jackie French. *Fish Fry Tonight*. Illustrated by Catherine O'Niell. Crown, 1992.

A cumulative tale in which Mouse catches a fish and then invites a large group of her friends to share it. The guest list grows until there are so many guests that she orders out for 100 pizzas.

Leedy, Loreen. *The Potato Party and Other Troll Tales*. Holiday House, 1989.

The trolls are so tired of potatoes, but the cave is full of them. They finally cook them all and invite guests to a wonderful party. All the potatoes are consumed, but later the party guests bring by a "thank you" gift—a whole sled of potatoes! There are other troll tales in this collection.

Munsch, Robert. *Moira's Birthday*. Illustrated by Michael Martchenko. Annick, 1987.

Moira invites her whole school to her birthday party, despite her parents' wishes. This resourceful girl comes up with more than enough food, cakes, and pizza to share.

Penner, Lucille Recht. *The Tea Party Book*. Illustrated by Jody Wheeler. Random House, 1993.

This book describes nine different tea parties, from Teddy Bears to Royal Tea to Rainy Day Tea. With lots of details on tea sets and treats, this charming book will stir the fantasies of anyone who loves to dress up and go to a tea party.

Shaw, Nancy. *Sheep Out to Eat*. Illustrated by Margot Apple. Houghton Mifflin, 1992.

Shaw's sheep are dining out. Their fluffy, funny misunderstandings, their trip to dinner, and their attempts to order food are described in hysterically understated rhyme. They even put pepper on their chocolate cake. Finally, they are asked to leave. What they really want to eat is the green grass on the lawn outside. They eat their fill and even leave a tip.

Shelby, Ann. *Potluck*. Illustrated by Irene Travis. Orchard, 1991.

Alpha and Betty have a potluck and invite all their friends, from A (Acton) to Z (Zeke and Zelda). Acton brings asparagus soup, Ben brings bagels, and so on through the alphabet.

Stadler, John. *Animal Café*. Macmillan, 1986.

Casey the cat and Sedgewick the dog keep their owner's food shop in business by operating an animal café once a week, after store hours. The owner never knows why his cash drawer is full those next mornings.

Stevenson, James. *Fried Feathers for Thanksgiving.* Greenwillow, 1986.

Dolores and Lavina Witch want to have a clean house and a turkey dinner for Thanksgiving. They trick Emma and her friends into cleaning the house. Then they sneak up on Emma as she makes stew, but several of Emma's animal friends combine to form a huge monster and scare the two witches away. Everyone in the forest has a happy Thanksgiving.

Tobias, Tobi. *Pot Luck.* Illustrated by Nola Langner Malone. Lothrop, Lee and Shepard, 1993.

Because Rachel's grandmother's friend Sophie comes to dinner on short notice, she will get "potluck." However, Rachel and her grandmother prepare a big meal: soup, roasted chicken, and homemade cake, with all the loving touches one adds for good friends.

Related Activities

Order Up!

This story about mixed up orders can be enacted on a flannel board while it is read. Make cutouts of the customers (Giraffe, Chameleon, Camel, Penguin, and Monkey) and the ice cream treats (soda, rainbow sherbet, bowl with two scoops of ice cream, malt, and banana split). A Cow puppet and a Sheep puppet can lead the children in calling out "Order up!"

It was a busy afternoon at the Chill and Grill Café. Cow had made one ice cream treat after another. Sheep had been serving customers all day, and his brain was tired. He could hardly remember who ordered what. But more customers kept coming and sitting on the stools at the soda counter. So Sheep kept serving them.

Giraffe sat on the first stool and Sheep took his order. "I'll have a giant-size chocolate chip soda. Bring that with a long, tall straw."

Sheep said, "Coming right up." And he ordered the giant-size chocolate chip soda for Giraffe.

Chameleon sat on the second stool and Sheep took his order. "I'll have a tiny dish of rainbow sherbet."

Sheep said, "Coming right up." And he ordered the tiny dish of rainbow sherbet for Chameleon.

Camel sat on the third stool and Sheep took his order. "I'll have a bowl with a double scoop of ice cream. Make one scoop rocky road and make the other peanut brittle Crunch."

Sheep said, "Coming right up." And he ordered the double scoop of ice cream for Camel.

Penguin sat on the fourth stool and Sheep took his order. "I'll have a mango malt in a chilled glass."

Sheep said, "Coming right up." And he ordered the mango malt for Penguin.

Monkey sat on the fifth stool and Sheep took his order. "I'll have a banana split."

Sheep said, "Coming right up." And he ordered the banana split for Monkey.

"Order up!" called Cow.

Sheep picked up the giant-size chocolate chip soda with the extra long straw and gave it to Chameleon.

Chameleon started to say, "Hold it! I think you've made a—"

"Order up!" called Cow.

Sheep picked up the tiny dish of rainbow sherbet and gave it to Camel.

Camel started to say, "Hold it! I think you've made a—"

"Order up!" called Cow.

Sheep picked up the bowl with a double scoop of ice cream and gave it to Penguin.

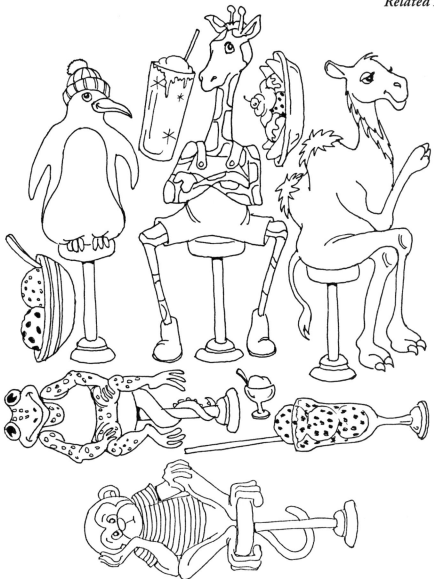

Penguin started to say, "Hold it! I think you've made a—"

"Order up!" called Cow.

Sheep picked up the mango malt in a chilled glass and gave it to Monkey.

Monkey started to say, "Hold it! I think you've made a—"

"Order up!" called Cow.

Sheep picked up the banana split and gave it to giraffe.

Giraffe looked at his order and said, "Hold it! I think you've made a—"

And all the customers at the counter yelled, "MISTAKE!"

"Hold on," said Sheep. "I can make everything right. Monkey, just pass that mango malt in a chilled glass to Penguin."

So Penguin got his mango malt and that was just right.

"Now," said Sheep. "Penguin, pass the double scoop of ice cream to Camel."

So Camel got his double scoop of ice cream and that was just right.

"Now," said Sheep. "Camel, pass the rainbow sherbet to Chameleon."

So Chameleon got his rainbow sherbet and that was just right.

"Now," said Sheep. "Chameleon, pass the chocolate chip soda to Giraffe."

So Giraffe got his chocolate chip soda and that was just right.

Monkey said, "Wait a minute. I don't have any ice cream at all!"

So Sheep took the banana split from Giraffe and gave it to Monkey. "Order Up!" called Sheep.

And as soon as all the customers at the counter finished their ice cream and left, Cow and Sheep hung the CLOSED sign on the door. It had been a very busy day at the Chill and Grill Café!

Better Luck Next Time

Characters

Andrews Family

Mom
Dad
Allison
Aaron

Zieman Family

Mom
Dad
Zelda
Zack

Two Narrators

Stage setup: Arrange eight chairs or stools in two straight lines (four chairs each) facing each other, yet angled so all characters can be seen by the audience. A narrator stands at each side. The families face each other.

Readers Theater scripts are not meant to be memorized, but read with animation. After parts are assigned, let children read over the script to get a sense of the characters they will play. For the performance, children can stand or be seated on stools. Occasionally, a character moves from one place to another (this is indicated in the script), but, in general, characters use body language to express emotions and action. For this script, the families move their stools closer together when the dinner begins.

Narrator 1: The Andrews family and the Zeimans had been neighbors and dinner companions for more than 10 years. Each Friday night they had a dinner exchange.

Narrator 2: A dinner exchange worked like this: On the first Friday of the month, both families ate at the Andrews' house. On the next Friday both families ate at the Zeiman's. Then the next Friday, they went back to the Andrews', and then the next Friday, to the Zeiman's. After that, the next Friday—

Narrator 1: I think that explains it.

Narrator 2: Sometimes the Andrews family would make all the food and sometimes the Zeimans would make all the food. Sometimes they each brought part of the meal. For example, last month, on the first Friday of the month, the Andrews family fixed a big pot of chili for both families and they also made a big pan of brownies to go with it. The next Friday, the Zeiman family made a pot of minestrone, a pot of spaghetti, and served dishes of spumoni ice cream. And on the next Friday, they planned a German dinner. The Andrews family brought sauerbraten and the Zeimans brought a German chocolate cake. Then the next Friday night—

Narrator 1: I think that explains it. And brings us up to date. This particular week, the families will be meeting at the Andrews' house.

Mom Andrews: I think we agreed to have a Mexican meal this Friday. We are doing the main course. What shall we have?

Allison Andrews: Let's have tacos.

Aaron Andrews: I like enchiladas.

Dad Andrews: Give me fajitas.

Mom Andrews: Let's just do tacos. Everybody likes that.

Dad Andrews: I'll get the ingredients at the store this week. We'll need taco shells, lettuce, tomatoes, ground beef, taco sauce, sour cream.

Allison Andrews: And cheese. Cheese. Lots of cheese!

Aaron Andrews: Please!

Mom Andrews: Okay, we're all set. We'll have Mexican food with the Zeimans this Friday night.

Narrator 2: Over at the Zeiman house there was preparation for Friday night, too.

Dad Zeiman: I'm sure we agreed to have Chinese this Friday night. We are bringing soup and dessert.

Mom Zeiman: Are you sure it was Chinese? I thought we were having Italian again.

Zack Zeiman: We're having pizza.

Zelda Zeiman: No. We were going to have tacos.

Zack Zeiman: Oh, stuff it. I'm sure it was pizza.

Dad Zeiman: Well, I'm sure it was Chinese.

Mom Zeiman: We could have egg drop soup. But what about dessert?

Zelda Zeiman and Zack Zeiman: Fortune cookies!

Dad Zeiman: This will be easy. All I need to buy is the broth and a dozen eggs. And I guess it doesn't matter if I drop them.

Zelda Zeiman: Oh, Dad. How corny.

Mom Zeiman: We're all set for Chinese on Friday night.

Narrator 1: Friday night came. Each family had shopped and cooked for the meal. Finally it was time to meet at the Andrews' house.
(The families move their stools closer together.)

Mom Andrews: Come in. My, that soup smells good. Let's eat right away.

Narrator 2: So the families sat down and Dad Zeiman uncovered the pot of soup.

Dad Zeiman: It's egg drop soup. All I needed was broth and a dozen eggs. And I guess it didn't matter if I dropped them.

Zelda Zeiman: Oh, Dad. That is so corny.

Mom Andrews: Egg drop soup?

Allison Andrews: Doesn't sound very Mexican to me.

Mom Zeiman: Mexican?

Zelda Zeiman: I told you so!

Dad Andrews: Well, I guess I'll spill the beans. To go with this egg drop soup, we are having tacos.

Mom Zeiman: Tacos?

Zack Zeiman: Doesn't sound very Chinese to me.

Aaron Andrews: I think somebody got mixed up.

Zelda Zeiman: I think everybody got mixed up.

Allison Andrews: What are we going to do?

Mom Andrews: I know. Why don't you freeze your soup and we can have it next week.

Zelda Zeiman: Then we'd have to listen to Dad's corny joke again.

Dad Andrews: Good point. We could freeze the tacos, but frozen lettuce and tomatoes never defrost very well.

Mom Andrews: What can we do?

Zack Zeiman: We can order out for pizza!

Mom Zeiman: Well, "potluck" means enjoying whatever has been cooked. Let's just eat.

Narrator 2: So they enjoyed the egg drop soup and had fun making tacos.

Narrator 1: Then it was time for dessert.

Zelda Zeiman and Zack Zeiman: Fortune cookies!

Narrator 2: Each person cracked open a cookie and read the fortune out loud.

Mom Andrews: Mine says: Better luck next time.

Zack Zeiman: Listen to this one: Next Friday night you will order pizza.

Aaron Andrews: You're making that one up.

Mom Zeiman: This is good: Confusion is the beginning of greater understanding and cooperation.

Dad Andrews: Here's an old Chinese fortune: That's the way the cookie crumbles.

Narrator 1: But the best fortune of all was Dad Zeiman's.

Dad Zeiman: He who drops eggs is surely destined to make egg drop soup.

Zelda Zeiman: Dad, that is so corny!

Other Activities

What's on the Menu?

The purpose of the menu is not only to list the dishes available but to make them look as appetizing as possible. Challenge pairs or small groups of children to choose a favorite type of restaurant and make a menu for it. This can be a specialty restaurant (such as a pizza parlor), a general café, or a fanciful restaurant in outer space or in a jungle.

Give each group two pieces of heavy paper, 11 by 14 inches. They decide how to fold and assemble the menu. The pictures for the menu can be drawn or cut from magazines and newspaper ads. The group will decide how many items are to be on the menu and which ones will have the most appealing pictures. Each item should have a brief description and a price.

Cover the completed menus with clear self-adhesive paper and then display them.

Waiting for the Waiter

Is there anything more boring in a restaurant than waiting for the food to come? Many restaurants have special place mats with games and jokes on them to help pass the time. Encourage children to be inventive and create their own. On 11-by-14-inch paper, have children lay out games such as word searches and dot to dots. They may also include riddles, face outlines to fill in, dinner-table game suggestions, and the beginnings of stories to finish. When these place mats are done, photocopy them and give several different ones to each child. They may use them at dinners out with their families.

Tea Party Song

(To the tune of "My Bonnie Lies Over the Ocean")

Young girls love to plan tea parties. Hopefully, they will invite boys, too, though this may not be of great importance to them. The American Girls collection of books by Pleasant Company describes five girls from different historical periods who loved tea parties. Libraries and schools are promoting tea party events built around the popularity of these books that introduce the conventions of tea parties and good manners. This song comes from these ideas and can be used with tea party programs.

We're having a party at teatime
We're having a party for fun,
I've set out my very best dishes,
Oh come join my party—just come

Join me, sit down,
Join me for teatime, Please come for tea
Dress up, Sit down,
Oh come have a party with me!

I'm serving treats made from my kitchen,
Sandwiches, cookies, and cake,
I've set out my very best dishes,
Which kind would you most like to take?

Join me, sit down,
Join me for teatime, Please come for tea
Dress up, Sit down,
Oh come have a party with me!

I'm bringing my dolls dressed in
    bonnets,
I'm bringing my brown teddy bear,
I'm bringing my stuffed dogs and
    kittens,
Please won't you take this little chair?

Join me, sit down,
Join me for teatime, Please come for tea
Dress up, Sit down,
Oh come have a party with me!

I'm using my very best manners,
"Thank you" and "please" are my style,
I know friends will always remember,
And treat me with hugs and a smile.

Join me, sit down,
Join me for teatime, Please come for tea
Dress up, Sit down,
Oh come have a party with me!

You Have Never Seen Anything Like It Before!

Every Sunday, colorful ads for all kinds of food spill out of the newspaper. Many of these are thrown away. Encourage recycling of these ads with a group project—make new ads for new products. These new sensations look like the same old things, but ... they have some magic property or surprising power. Take a picture ad featuring the lowly potato and transform it into a plug for Super Spud, the Potato of Champions!

To extend this activity, have groups of children create stories about what happens when these unusual products are taken home.

Starter Kit

The "Out of the Carry-Out Box" Starter Kit will provide a visual aid that will introduce your food theme or unit quickly. No one can resist wondering what is inside a bag or basket so just setting it on a display or holding it up will attract attention. The items inside the container will introduce the "flavor" of the food theme and start imaginations racing. In addition, many of the items will be used in specific activities or stories, so it is easy for you to assemble. It's all in the bag!

For this dining-in-and-eating-out food theme, you might pack these items into a chicken bucket or a few carry-out containers for Chinese food:

> assorted menus from a variety of fast food and formal restaurants
> colorful ads for the activity "You Have Never Seen Anything Like It Before!"
> copy of the focus book *Chicken Sunday*
> assorted ice cream containers such as a soda glass or sundae dish and a copy of the story "Order Up!"
> toy tea party set
> paper and cloth napkins
> party favors such as nut cups
> paper and markers to design menus and place mats
> transparency of the "Tea Party Song"

Also for this theme, you might prepare individual fast food bags with copies of place mats from fast-food restaurants children can design and sample mats suggested in the activity "Waiting for the Waiter."

Recipes

Better-Luck-Next-Time Egg Drop Soup

Good for Taking to a Potluck or for When You Have Guests

INGREDIENTS:
1 can CHICKEN BROTH
2 CUPS WATER
1 Teaspoon SALT
1 SLICE GINGER ROOT (OPTIONAL)
1 GREEN ONION, SLICED
2 EGGS

METHOD:

BETTER LUCK NEXT TIME EGG DROP SOUP

1. MIX CHICKEN BROTH, WATER, and SALT in a PAN.
2. ADD the GINGER ROOT SLICE IF YOU WISH.
3. BRING the MIXTURE to a BOIL. REMOVE the GINGER ROOT SLICE.
4. In a BOWL, BEAT EGGS with a FORK or a WIRE WHISK.
5. STIR EGGS into the HOT MIXTURE in the PAN.
6. IMMEDIATELY REMOVE the PAN from HEAT.
7. POUR the SOUP into INDIVIDUAL SOUP BOWLS.
8. ADD a FEW SLICES of GREEN ONION to EACH SOUP BOWL for a GARNISH.

Tea Punch

INGREDIENTS:

3 Tea BAGS
4 CUPS COOL WATER
2 CUPS JUICE (CRANBERRY-APPLE or ORANGE-CRANBERRY)
3 Teaspoons SUGAR
ORANGE

METHOD:

Tea PUNCH

1. measure 2 CUPS of the WATER into a PAN and BRING to a BOIL.
2. Remove the pan from HEAT and ADD Tea BAGS. LET STAND 5 minutes. Remove Tea BAGS.
3. ADD the Remaining 2 CUPS of COOL WATER.
4. POUR the Tea into a PITCHER and ADD JUICE.
5. STIR in SUGAR.
6. SLICE the ORANGE.
7. POUR Tea PUNCH into Tea CUPS, and ADD an ORANGE SLICE to each CUP.

Cucumber Sandwich

INGREDIENTS:

2 SLICES BREAD
2 TEASPOONS BUTTER or MARGARINE
6 CUCUMBERS

METHOD:

CUCUMBER SANDWICH

1. SPREAD 1 TEASPOON of MARGARINE on EACH of 2 SLICES of BREAD.
2. SLICE CUCUMBER and PLACE on the BUTTERED SIDE of 1 SLICE of BREAD, LAY the OTHER SLICE of BREAD on TOP, BUTTERED SIDE DOWN.
3. TRIM CRUSTS, IF YOU WISH. SLICE the SANDWICH into 4 SMALL SQUARES.

Ham-Spread Sandwiches

INGREDIENTS:

2 SLICES BREAD
½ CUP DEVILED HAM
1 TABLESPOON CELERY
½ TEASPOON mayonnaise

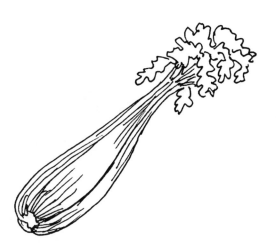

METHOD:

HAM-SPREAD SANDWICH

1. CHOP CELERY and ADD to the DEVILED HAM.
2. IN a BOWL, mIX mayonnaise into the DEVILED HAM and CELERY.
3. SPREAD on 1 SLICE of BREAD. COVER with another SLICE of BREAD.
4. TRIM CRUSTS, IF YOU WISH. CUT the SANDWICH into 4 SMALL TRIANGLES.

Chapter 6

Out of the Cake Box

Introduction

Just-out-of-the-oven pies, cakes, cookies, and breads fill this chapter. Another tasty topic is ice cream and all the trimmings.

Bread is a basic in the diet of much of the world. Phrases like "our daily bread," "bread and butter," and even "bread winner" show its essentiality. Bread is part of many cultures, symbolizing community and friendship as well as nourishment.

Our language is full of food expressions about baked goods. "Easy as pie," and "piece of cake" indicate that a task will be accomplished easily. Many current picture books reflect an unfailing interest in baked goods and bakeries. Very few picture books about nutritional foods are published. It is just not as much fun to write a book about bean curd!

Cakes are a favorite topic for picture books, from Patricia Polacco's *Thunder Cake* to the traditional rhyme *Pat-a-Cake*. *Ruth's Bake Shop* is a virtual catalog of cakes, pies, and other sweets. Many of the treats listed in this chapter can be used to introduce cultures around the world. At many times during the year, particularly at holiday time, baked goods become part of important traditions. Supplement this chapter with ethnic cookbooks listed in the Resource Bibliography and make kringla from Norway or bunuelos from Mexico.

Kids have a vested interest in this topic: They like sweets. Much of the preparation of baked goods can include children, especially stirring and licking the bowl. And what food is more important than that annual birthday cake. Generations of picture takers have made it possible to have your cake and eat it too!

This chapter's focus book, *The Doorbell Rang*, offers opportunities for math activities (dividing a set number of cookies as more children arrive), as well as discussions of sharing and decision making when faced with limited amount of food.

Baking from scratch can teach many math concepts in very concrete terms. Skills that can be taught in this "hands on" way include measuring, doubling, sequencing, and classification. Even reluctant readers will decipher instructions when the result will be something good to eat.

Focus Book

The Doorbell Rang, by Pat Hutchins. Greenwillow, 1986.

Ma makes one dozen cookies for Sam and Victoria, but the doorbell rings. Tom and Hannah from next door come inside to share the cookies. The doorbell rings again. Next come Peter and his little brother. The doorbell rings repeatedly until 12 children are present to share the dozen cookies. The doorbell rings one last time. Everyone is relieved and delighted to see Grandma with an enormous tray of fresh cookies.

Focus Book Activities

Spoken Expression

After the story is read to the children, invite them to act it out while the story is read a second time. Assign the parts of Mom, Grandma, Sam, Victoria, Tom, Hannah, Peter, Peter's little brother, Joy, Simon, and the four cousins to children in your class or library. Make a name tag or sign for each character and give each one a paper plate for the cookies. Use real cookies or construction-paper shapes.

Spoken Expression

Ask children to describe the characters' feelings at different points in the story. How do Sam and Victoria feel at the beginning, at the end of the story, and just before Grandma comes with the tray of cookies?

Spoken and Written Expression

Read the story again, up to the point where Grandmother comes with the tray of cookies. Ask children to rewrite the ending. What if Grandmother does not show up with the cookies? How might the story end? This ending could be written as a group story or acted out impromptu with characters becoming fussy and argumentative.

Math Connection

This story can be used as a math exercise since children are asked to divide the 12 cookies into two, three, and four parts. Write this as a word problem. Have children make up other stories that involve dividing, subtracting, and adding. Food stories are good examples. Children might write a pie story or a cake story that also uses division or introduces the concepts of greater than and less than.

Written Expression

Remind children that the mother in Hutchins' book says "No one makes cookies like Grandma's." Have children make cookie-shape books and write stories about a Grandma who makes the best cookies in the world.

Spoken Expression

Role play the parts of different characters. Have someone act out the part of the mother. How does she feel about the growing trail of footprints on the floor she is trying to mop?

Longer Read Aloud Book

McCloskey, Robert. *Homer Price*. Viking, 1943. 149 pages.

Homer Price is a boy with a knack for finding mysteries and solving them. This book has six short adventures, including "The Donuts"—a doughnut machine gets a mind of its own.

Related Titles

Asch, Frank. *Milk and Cookies*. Parent's Magazine Press, 1982.

While staying at Grandpa and Grandma's house, Baby Bear dreams about feeding milk and cookies to a dragon.

Brimmer, Larry Dave. *Country Bear's Good Neighbor*. Illustrated by Ruth Tietjen Councell. Orchard, 1988.

Country Bear borrows all the ingredients for a cake from his good neighbor. Just when the neighbor decides she has been asked to lend too much, Country Bear rewards the generous young girl with a gift of apple-cinnamon-walnut cake. The recipe is included at the end.

Czernecki, Stefan. *The Sleeping Bread*. Hyperion, 1992.

Beto owns a bakery shop in the village of San Pedro, Guatemala, and he feeds Zafiro, a beggar who is avoided by most people in the village. When Zafiro decides to leave, he sheds a tear into the baker's water jug, and, overnight, the bread stops rising. Everyone tries to help, but only when the beggar returns and washes away the tears does Beto's bread rise again. Brilliantly colored folk art designs make the book a visual treat.

dePaola, Tomie. *Tony's Bread*. Putnam, 1989.

This fanciful book traces the origin of "poettone," a sweet, Italian bread. Tony is a baker with one daughter. Though she is old enough to marry, Tony does not allow her to even speak to an eligible man. Then one day, rich Angelo comes to town and falls in love with the bread and the daughter. Angelo's plot to marry the daughter brings good fortune to Tony and fame to his bread.

Dragonwagon, Crescent. *This Is the Bread I Baked for Ned*. Illustrated by Isadore Seltzer. Macmillan, 1989.

In this cumulative story, a woman bakes bread, makes salad and soup, and prepares the table for Ned's supper. Ned arrives with 13 friends! Fortunately, there is enough to go around and all the guests clean up after they eat. The story is told in rhyme, with clear pictures of each food item.

Dunbar, Joyce. *A Cake for Barney*. Illustrated by Emilie Boon. Orchard, 1987.

Barney Bear has a cake with five cherries on it. Barney cannot eat it, because various animals keep coming along asking for a cherry. Finally, all the cherries are gone, but then a bully bear tries to take the cake. Barney keeps his cake by eating it!

Edwards, Michelle. *A Baker's Portrait*. Lothrop, Lee & Shephard, 1991.

Michelin the artist is invited to paint a portrait of her fat aunt and uncle, the bakers. She has always painted truthfully, even if the results were not flattering. She hates to hurt their feelings, but she knows she must paint honestly. After much struggle, she paints a picture that portrays the couple as their nicknames for each other: Chocolate Cake and Crusty Challah (a Jewish holiday roll).

Heath, Amy. *Sophie's Role.* Illustrated by Shelia Hamanaka. Four Winds, 1992.

Sophie helps behind the counter at her parents' bakery on a busy day—the day before Christmas. The text richly describes the sounds at the busy bakery, and the illustrations glowingly portray the rich cakes, breads, and cookies. The story is told from young Sophie's sprightly perspective.

Hennessy, B.G. *Jake Baked the Cake.* Illustrated by Mary Morgan. Viking, 1990.

All the preparations for a wedding are described in rhyming text. Jake the Baker makes the crowning touch: a magnificent four-tier wedding cake.

Janovitz, Marilyn. *Pat-a-Cake.* Hyperion, 1992.

The pat-a-cake rhyme is illustrated with pictures of a mother goose and its baby getting a special cake from a pig's bakery. There are lusciously detailed goodies on every page.

Kent, Jack. *Ice Cream Soup.* Illustrated by R. W. Alley. Random House, 1990.

A brother and sister are so fascinated with events that happen on their way home from the grocery store that the ice cream they are carrying turns to ice cream soup.

Lee, Dennis. *Ice Cream Store.* Illustrated by David McPhail. Scholastic, 1992.

This collection includes several poems about food. "The Ice Cream Store" is a good poem for introducing multicultural activities. Also included are "Shake-n-Bake a Jelly," "Popping Popcorn," and "Batty Betty Cooks Spaghetti."

Lindsey, Treka. *When Batistine Made Bread.* Macmillan, 1985.

Six-year-old Batistine lived in the Old Country a long time ago, when baking bread involved harvesting and thrashing the wheat, mixing the "meal" flour, kneading, and baking. In clear language that modern children will understand, this story describes the method of truly making bread from scratch.

Macdonald, Maryann. *Hedgehog Bakes a Cake.* Illustrated by Lynn Munsinger. Bantam, 1990.

As Hedgehog begins to make a cake, Rabbit, Squirrel, and Owl stop by, one at a time, to advise the preparations. After they leave, Hedgehog begins all over, following the recipe, to turn out a perfect cake. A recipe for Hedgehog's cake is included at the end.

Mayer, Marianna. *Marcel, the Pastry Chef.* Bantam Books, 1991.

Marcel creates goodies that make dessert into an art form. Clear pictures and simple text describe the busy day of this specialized cook.

Munsch, Robert. *Moira's Birthday.* Illustrated by Michael Martchenko. Annick, 1987.

Moira invites her whole school to her birthday party, despite her parents' wishes. This resourceful girl comes up with more than enough food, cakes, and pizza to share.

Murphy, Jill. *A Piece of Cake.* Putnam, 1989.

When Mama Elephant goes on a diet she puts the whole family on one, too. Then Granny sends a cake, and no one can resist just one piece.

Polacco, Patricia. *Thunder Cake.* Putnam, 1990.

The young girl is frightened of the coming storm until her grandmother teaches her to make Thunder Cake. As they gather the ingredients and mix the cake, the girl forgets the storm. When the thunder cracks overhead, they are eating the first piece.

Robart, Rose. *Cake That Mac Ate.* Illustrated by Maryann Kovalski. Little, Brown, 1986.

In this cumulative tale reminiscent of "This Is the House That Jack Built," we learn the sequence of events in making the cake that Mac ate. Mac, incidentally, is the family dog, and Mac's owners are horrified by his actions.

Shalev, Meir. *My Father Always Embarrasses Me.* Illustrated by Yossi Abolafia. Wellington Publishing, 1990.

Mortimer is embarrassed by his stay-at-home father's eccentric ways until his dad makes the winning cake at the class baking contest.

Spohn, Kate. *Ruth's Bake Shop.* Orchard, 1990.

Ruth, an octopus, makes a list of cleaning chores she needs to do, but instead of doing them she buys ingredients to bake the things she wants: a wide assortment of cookies, pies, bread, pastries, and cakes. After she bakes, Ruth does her cleaning and then opens a bake shop.

Spurr, Elizabeth. *The Biggest Birthday Cake.* Illustrated by Rosanne Litzinger. Harcourt Brace Jovanovich, 1991.

The richest-and-fattest man in the world orders an enormous birthday cake when he turns 40. At first, he wants to keep it all for himself, but when he falls into the icing and children save him, he decides to share the cake. Then he also becomes the happiest man in the world.

Taylor, Judy. *Dudley Bakes a Cake.* Illustrated by Peter Cross. Putnam, 1988.

It is the day of Shadyhanger Faire and Dudley, a door mouse, decides to bake a cake for a contest to win a fancy bike. When Dudley discovers he doesn't have enough carrots for the cake, he adds extra baking powder. The cake grows so big the stove explodes. Dudley adds strawberry icing and hauls it to the fair. After he wins the grand prize, a swarm of bees takes over the cake and carries it away.

Wellington, Monica. *Mr. Cookie Baker.* Dutton, 1992.

In this well-designed book, each page is bordered with cookies, cookie cutters, or kitchen utensils. The brief text describes the work of Mr. Baker, who makes the cookies that are sold by Mrs. Baker in the bakeshop. Recipes for cookies and frosting are included in the back of the book.

Wells, Rosemary. *Max's Chocolate Chicken.* Dial, 1989.

Wells' roly-poly bunnies, Max and Ruby, celebrate Easter with an egg hunt. The one who finds the most eggs will win a chocolate chicken. Ruby finds all the eggs while Max plays, but then Max hides with the chocolate chicken and eats it as Ruby searches for him. In the end, Max has a dirty face and Ruby is rewarded with a chocolate duck.

Wild, Jocelyn. *Eric and Florence Take the Cake.* Dial, 1987.

Florence and Eric, two lambs, spend the summer at Granny and Grandpa Mutton's. They are sent on an errand to pick up a cake at Lavinia Bleating's house. In the meantime, Lavinia's sister, Muriel, buys a new hat and leaves it, still in its box, on the hall table, next to the cake, which is also in a box. Cake and hat get mixed up, with disastrous results.

Wolfe, Ferida. *Seven Loaves of Bread.* Illustrated by Katie Keller. Tambourine, 1993.

When the farm's usual baker gets sick, Rose discovers there are very good reasons to make extra loaves of bread to share with friends.

Ziefert, Harriet. *Chocolate Mud Cake.* Illustrated by Karen Gundersheimer. Harper & Row, 1988.

Molly and Jenny, her little sister, play in Grandma's yard and pretend that they are making a yummy cake out of lumps of dirt, water, sand, nuts, berries, and leaves. They bake it in the sun and create a chocolate mud cake Grandma and Grandpa will enjoy.

Ziegler, Sandra. *A Visit to the Bakery.* Children's Press, 1987.

Clear photographs follow a school class on a tour of the bakery to see the steps in mixing and baking bread.

Related Activities

The Six Bickering Bread Bakers

To follow up the telling of this bread story, serve samples of the different breads: French, sourdough, cinnamon-raisin, banana, seven-grain, and whole wheat. Cut the bread into bite-size pieces and let children play the parts of different bakers, each trying to convince the others that his or her bread is the best.

Once there were six bakers who were good friends. They had always dreamed of opening the finest bakery in town. Because they were all such good bakers, they were sure the bakery would be a success.

Each baker made a special kind of bread. Françoise made French, Sam made sourdough, Cindy Rae made cinnamon-raisin, Anna made banana, Seth Solomon made seven-grain, and Wally made plain whole wheat.

"This is a great idea!" said Wally. "Good bakers, good friends! What could be better?"

Well the bakers all remained good bakers, but they soon began to bicker. They could not agree on what to name their bakery or even what kind of bread they should make.

Françoise said, "But of course, my French bread will be the most popular. It is crusty on the outside, and warm and soft on the inside. The recipe is straight from the finest chef in Paris. But of course, we must make French bread!"

"What?" said Cindy Rae. "French bread is boring. People want sweet and spicy breads like my cinnamon-raisin. People want a bread that is pretty to look at and tasty, too. Cinnamon-raisin must be our bread."

Seth disagreed. "Healthy bread! That is what people want. My seven-grain is sure to sell and sell. It is nutritious and very good for you. We must have seven-grain!"

Anna said, "What good is 'good for you' if it is not tasty too? My banana bread has fruit in it, and is sweet and tasty. No other bread will do. We must have banana bread."

Sam grumbled, "I never expected to agree with you, anyway. My sourdough is certainly the most unique and we must make it. This bakery will never work, anyway."

"Oh, Sam, don't give up yet," said Wally, "Everyone has a special contribution. Françoise's French bread is crusty and warm. Just right for supper on Wednesday, with a big plate of spaghetti. Anna's banana bread is tasty, and perfect for breakfast on Tuesday. Sam, your sourdough is good with fish on Friday. Cindy Rae's cinnamon-raisin makes a wonderful Saturday-morning treat. That seven-grain bread of Seth's makes a great, super-healthy sandwich for lunch on Thursday."

Anna said, "That is a bread for every day of the week. What a good idea."

Seth said, "We'll have a special bread each day!"

Sam said, "I don't think this is going to work. We don't have a bread for Monday—the first day of the week."

Cindy Rae said, "Oh, yes, we do, Sam. We have 'Start the Week with Wally's Whole Wheat.'"

Wally said, "I like that, Cindy Rae. I'd be honored to have my bread featured. This is a great idea. Good bakers, good friends! What could be better?"

Sam's sour face slowly broke into a smile. "All week, good friends bake bread together. Good friends should also break bread together. On Sunday, let's share brunch at my house."

A Cake Fit for a Queen

Characters

Queen
Giraffe
Hippo
Peacock
Sloth
Monkey
Prince
Herald

Two Narrators

Stage setup: Arrange eight chairs or stools in a line or semicircle; a narrator sits at each end, and the contestants are seated with the Queen in the middle. Herald stands off to one side. Prince sits behind the Queen's stool until it is time for his part.

Readers Theater scripts are not meant to be memorized, but read with animation. After parts are assigned, let children read over the scripts to get a sense of the characters they will play. For the performance, children can stand or be seated on stools. Occasionally, a character moves from one place to another (this is indicated in the script), but, in general, characters use body language to express emotions and action. For this script, contestants can stir their cakes and bow to the Queen when presenting them.

Narrator 1: In the land of Tort 'n Crumpet the Good Queen was celebrating a special day. Early in the morning, the royal herald made an announcement.

Herald: Today is a very special day for the Queen, and she is holding a cake contest. The winner will make a cake that will amaze the Queen, a cake that will delight the Queen, a cake fit for a Queen.

Narrator 2: All her subjects rushed off to their kitchens to bake cakes.

Narrator 1: Giraffe went right to work.

Giraffe: I know what will amaze and delight the Queen. I'll make a cake with 50 layers. It will be as tall as I am.

Narrator 2: So Giraffe baked a 50-layer cake for the Queen.

Narrator 1: Hippo went right to work, too.

Hippo: I know what will amaze and delight the Queen. I'll make the fattest, roundest cake ever seen. I usually make a pound cake, but this time I'll make a 100-pound cake. I'll make a cake that is as fat as I am.

Narrator 2: So Hippo baked a round, fat cake for the Queen.

Narrator 1: Peacock went right to work, too.

Peacock: I know what will amaze and delight the Queen. I'll make a cake with icing an inch thick. There will be pink roses and yellow roses everywhere. It will be as fancy and colorful as I am.

Narrator 2: So Peacock baked a fancy cake with lots of roses on top for the Queen.

Narrator 1: Sloth took a nap and then slowly went to work.

Sloth: I know what will amaze and delight the Queen. I'll make a cake that is most unusual. The topping will be on the bottom, the bottom will be on the top. It will be as upside down as I am.

Narrator 2: So Sloth baked an upside down cake for the Queen.

Narrator 1: Monkey went right to work, too.

Monkey: I know what will amaze and delight the Queen. I'll make a cake with colored sprinkles, inside and out. It will be a funny cake, with a laugh in every bite. It will be as funny as I am.

Narrator 2: So Monkey baked a confetti cake for the Queen.

Narrator 1: At the end of the day, all the bakers gathered at the palace. The contest began with Giraffe.

Giraffe: Your Majesty, I brought you the tallest cake ever baked. Surely the tallest cake ever baked is fit for a queen.

Queen: That is indeed the tallest cake ever baked. It does delight and amaze me, but it is not quite fit for a queen.

Narrator 2: Hippo spoke next.

Hippo: Your Majesty, I brought you the roundest, fattest cake ever baked. Surely the roundest, fattest cake ever baked is fit for a queen.

Queen: That is indeed the roundest, fattest cake ever baked. It does delight and amaze me, but it is not quite fit for a queen.

Narrator 1: Then Peacock presented his cake.

Peacock: Your Majesty, I brought you the fanciest cake ever baked. Surely the fanciest cake ever baked is fit for a queen.

Queen: That is indeed the fanciest cake ever baked. It does delight and amaze me, but it is not quite fit for a queen.

Narrator 2: Slowly, Sloth came forward with his cake.

Sloth: Your Majesty, I brought you the most unusual cake ever baked. It is an upside down cake. Surely an upside down cake is fit for a queen.

Queen: That is indeed the most unusual cake ever baked. It does delight and amaze me, but it is not quite fit for a queen.

Narrator 1: Finally, Monkey brought forward his cake.

Monkey: Your Majesty, I brought you a cake with sprinkles, inside and out. I brought you the funniest cake ever baked. Surely the funniest cake ever baked is fit for a queen.

Queen: That is indeed the funniest cake ever baked. It does delight and amaze me, but it is not quite fit for a queen.

Narrator 2: There seemed to be no more cakes to present

Herald: What?! There are no cakes in all this land fit for a queen?

Narrator 1: Then from behind the throne came the little voice of the little Prince. (Prince crawls out to stand by the Queen.)

Prince: I have a cake. It's not tall or fat; it's not fancy or unusual or funny.

Queen: Let me see it.

Narrator 2: When the Queen saw the cake, she smiled a big smile. It was just a little chocolate cake, but on the top was written—

Queen: "Happy birthday, Mama."

Narrator 1: Because the Prince knew that the Queen's special day was her birthday.

Queen: This is indeed an amazing and delightful cake. This is indeed a cake fit for THIS queen.

Narrator 2: So everyone sang "Happy Birthday," and then they cut the cake.

Narrator 1: And the Queen gave the Prince the first piece.

Other Activities

Body Bread

This whole-body action chant can be done several ways. Divide the students into five groups. Teach one line of the chant and its accompanying actions to each group, and let them practice. Then do the chant with each group saying only the line they have practiced. As they know the parts better, say the chant faster. When they are secure with their words, have them do all five lines at the same time. After the children are familiar with the words and actions to the whole chant, do it as a round.

Stir, stir, stir the dough
(said briskly, children seated performing stirring actions)

Knead it, knead it
(elongate the "e" sound in the word "knead," children on their knees performing kneading actions)

Punch it down, punch it down
(say "punch" emphatically, children stand up and punch their fists into their other pals, say "down," children squat)

Shape it, bake it
(children seated curling their arms around their bodies and tucking their heads in)

Eat it up!
(children jump up with their arms raised)

Cookie Exchange

Out of each of three different colors of paper, cut circles or other cookie shapes. Divide children into three groups. Each group gets one color of cookie shapes. One group invents characters for stories. They write one character name or description on each cookie. The second group invents actions, and the third, settings.

Have children exchange their cookies. Each group trades with the other two until it has equal numbers of character, action, and setting cookies. The groups then use their character, action, and setting cookies to create stories. Each group may develop one elaborate story, or several vignettes.

Share the stories orally, perhaps tape-recording them for later transcription.

Characters

giant
prince, princess
king, queen
knight
squire
crone
hermit
sage
wizard, sorceress
duke, duchess
lord, lady
lady in waiting
goatherd
goose girl
dairy maid
baker
stargazer
tailor
jester
farmer
alchemist

Actions

mix a potion
cast a spell
run away
hunt for a treasure
encounter a danger
solve a mystery
slay a dragon
joust

tell a story
go on a quest
ride a horse
sing songs
hide
chase a magic deer
explore a castle
enter a dark forest
go on a journey

Settings

castle
forest
cave
mountain
dungeon
battleground
hut
town square
remote village
cottage
bottom of the sea
above the clouds
edge of the world
forest glen
dovecote
courtyard
hearth
inn
bedchamber

Bake Sale

Write the names of animals on a set of index cards. Write the names of treats on another set. (See list below for starters.) Then have children match them. Read this introduction:

Here we are at the big bake sale. Lots of animals brought sweets to sell, but someone mixed up the labels. Can you match each animal with the sweet treat it made?

monkey—banana cream pie
goose—gooseberry pie
frog—shoo fly pie
mouse—cheese cake
sea horse—sponge cake
brown bear—brownies
rabbit—carrot cake
zebra—zucchini cake

dalmation—chocolate chip cake
poodle—torte
dachshund—shortcake
hyena—wacky cake
pig—mud pie
turkey—pumpkin pie
jellyfish—jelly roll

Have children make their own animal and treat cards to add to the sets.

A Month of Sundaes Calendar: (Writing and Art Activity)

This calendar can be used as a display for children to illustrate and brainstorm with before they create their own calendars. The teacher or librarian can first introduce and discuss the idiom "a month of Sundays." Then give children a calendar with 30 days each marked "Sunday" and ask them to invent a sundae dessert for each Sunday of the month.

Another way to use this calendar is to reproduce it on a large chart or an overhead transparency and then have children name the ingredients that would be used to make the sundaes. Notice that some sundaes simply play upon phrases such as "Yours 'til the milk shakes"; others, such as the "Hansel and Gretel Sundae," invite children to imagine what their favorite story-time character might make. Use these ideas and examples as springboards for writing, discussing, and imagining all the sweet possibilities.

1. Mud Slide Sundae
2. Lip-Smacking Licorice Sundae
3. Better than Double Chocolate Sundae
4. Here's Mud in Your Eye Sundae
5. Peach Pit Sundae
6. Banana Peel Sundae
7. Kumquat Kiss Sundae
8. Top Banana Toffee Sundae
9. It's the Berries Sundae
10. Yours 'til the Cookie Crumbles Sundae
11. Yours 'til the Milk Shakes Sundae
12. Georgia Peach Sundae
13. The George Washington Cherry Sundae
14. Fruit Basket Upset Sundae
15. Yours 'til the Banana Splits Sundae
16. Easy as Pie Sundae
17. No Pie à la Mode Sundae
18. Watermelon Seed Sundae
19. Shoo Fly Pie Sundae
20. Sugar Plum Sundae
21. Pigout Sundae
22. Proof of the Pudding Sundae
23. Cow Jumped over the Moon Sundae
24. Jack and Jill Sundae
25. Very Hungry Caterpillar Sundae
26. Gingerbread Boy Sundae
27. Hansel and Gretel Sundae
28. Hare and the Tortoise Sundae
29. Santa Claus' Favorite Sundae
30. Easter Bunny Sunday Sundae

A Month of Sundaes Calendar

Sundae Sundae Sundae Sundae Sundae Sundae Sundae

It's a Piece of ... Pie?

Bringing fractions to life is easy as pie with these verses that match the number of people with the amount of pie each person gets. Cut out circles of poster board, cut each circle into a different number of equal segments. Children choose group leaders —each holds a pie. A pie holder chooses a flavor that begins with the initial of his or her first name. Then the pie holder chooses as many children as there are pieces in that pie. Groups stand in different parts of the room and each group recites one verse following this model:

Charlie had a cherry pie.
He ate it all himself.
1 person, 1 whole pie.

Alice had an apple pie.
She shared it with one friend.
2 people, 1/2 pie each.

Barbara had a banana pie.
She shared it with two friends.
3 people, 1/3 pie each.

To expand this activity, write frames for these verses on paper, one for each group. They will look like this:

```
        had a        pie
S/he shared with     friend(s).
        people,      pie each.
```

Have each group complete a frame with its unique information. These can be compiled into a counting book about fractions. Photographs or self portraits of each group will enliven the pages.

31 More Flavors

Ice cream in 31 varieties? Only the beginning! Show the children a list of the flavors available in a local ice cream shop. Encourage them to let their imaginations fly for zany ice cream combinations. Children receive a triangle of paper to be the ice cream cone and as many circles as they have letters in their names. They choose (or invent) an ice cream flavor for each letter, and color the circles as the ice cream might look. For example, Amy might have apple, maple, and yogurt ice cream.

There are numerous ways to use these ice cream creations. Put each child's circles in an envelope. Collect the envelopes, shuffle, and pass them out. They must unscramble the letters and find out whose ice cream creation they have.

Have children bring their ice cream creations to small groups and share the kinds of ice cream chosen. (Vanilla is actually the most popular flavor, but not very many names have a "v" in them.) Can the group help those who are stumped on finding a flavor, such as one that begins with "e"?

Finally, these cones can be assembled and mounted on mural paper, adding glitter and confetti for toppings. Hang them in a room or a hall.

Starter Kit

The "Out of the Cake Box" Starter Kit will provide a visual aid that will introduce your food theme or unit quickly. No one can resist wondering what is inside a bag or basket, so just setting it on a display or holding it up will attract attention. The items inside the container will introduce the "flavor" of the food theme and start imaginations racing. In addition, many of the items will be used in specific activities or stories, so it is easy for you to assemble. It's all in the bag!

For this chapter's theme of bread, cakes, and sweets, you might pack these items into a bakery cake box or cake safe:

bakers' hats and aprons for the story "The Six Bickering Bread Bakers"
copy of the focus book *The Doorbell Rang*
thick paper circles cut into different numbers of equal segments for the "It's a Piece of ... Pie?" activity
copies of *Marcel, the Pastry Chef* and *Mr. Cookie Baker*
masks and a copy of the script "A Cake Fit for a Queen"
assorted baking utensils including baking and pie pans, loaf pans, measuring cups and spoons, rolling pin and cookie cutters, small bundt pan, and cookie sheets
tiny muffins, for a treat
cake mix
ice cream cone, ice cream scoop
copies of the recipe pages for each child
index cards for "Bake Sale" activity
paper cookie shapes for the activity "Cookie Exchange"
blank calendar pages for the activity "A Month of Sundaes Calendar"

Recipes

Good-and-Easy
Frozen Cherry-Banana Ice Cream Cups

INGREDIENTS:

1 21-ounce can cherry pie filling
1 pint vanilla ice cream
1 tablespoon lemon juice
3 bananas

METHOD:

GOOD-and-easy frozen CHERRY-Banana Ice cream CUPS

1. Soften Ice cream at room temperature. Spoon it into a mixing bowl.
2. Stir the cherry pie filling into the ice cream
3. Add lemon juice.
4. Chop the bananas, and add them to the mixture. Stir everything together. It will look like a thick ice cream soup.
5. Place paper baking cups in 12-muffin tins.
6. Spoon or pour the cherry-banana ice cream into the cups.
7. Freeze for several hours.
8. Before serving let the cups thaw at room temperature for several minutes.

Make-Bake-Take Cake

(to Grandma's House or to a Friend)

INGREDIENTS:

FOR CAKE:
1 Package of yellow cake mix
1 egg
½ C. orange juice (instead of water)

FOR GLAZE:
1¼ cups confectioner's sugar
¼ cup orange juice
1 teaspoon vanilla

METHOD:

make-bake-take-cake

FOR CAKE:
1. in a mixing bowl, blend cake mix, egg, and half the orange juice (instead of the water called for in the cake recipe).
2. Beat one minute with an electric mixer or a wooden spoon.
3. Add the rest of the orange juice, and beat the mixture for 3 more minutes.
4. Pour the mixture into a greased square 8-by-8-inch aluminum foil pan (so Grandma or a friend can keep it).
5. Bake for 20 minutes.
6. Cool for 15 minutes.

FOR GLAZE:
1. Sift confectioner's sugar into a mixing bowl (or mash up the lumps with a fork so it will mix easily with other ingredients).
2. Add the orange juice and vanilla
3. Beat with an electric mixer or a wooden spoon until the mixture is fairly smooth.
4. Pour over the top of the warm cake.
5. Put foil over the top of the cooled cake and take it to Grandma or to a friend!

Chapter 7

Out of the Soup Pot

Introduction

This chapter is about one-pot meals, including soups, stews, casseroles, and leftovers—anything that can be thrown together to make a meal in one pot. Historically, throughout the world, food has long been prepared in pots. It still is today, especially in many developing nations. People can always make a pot of soup, even without a microwave or an electrified kitchen. And, perhaps more than any other kind of food, soup is associated with nourishment. Soup is a symbol for food that heals the body and soothes the spirit. A sandwich can be just as nutritional, but the experience of eating soup is unique.

For kids, eating soup is fun. Slurping is fun! Chicken noodle soup and alphabet soup are very popular with children. Leftovers are sometimes unpopular with kids (casserole again?), but they are fun to complain about. Raiding the refrigerator is a hunt-and-find game with no adult direction on what to eat. Stew can be fun, too, especially when made over a campfire. One of the recipes in this chapter encourages children to make stew out of anything they have around.

Several books listed in the Related Titles section of this chapter use alphabet soup to introduce both a variety of foods and the letters of the alphabet. Other soup books are fun for different reasons. *Toni and the Tomato Soup* tells about a fussy eater who wants to eat tomato soup only. Too much of a good thing becomes a nightmare. Horace, the boy in *Mean Soup*, learns that making soup can help "stir away a bad day."

The focus book, *Alphabet Soup: A Feast of Letters*, stretches the imagination and expands the traditional associations for every letter of the alphabet. Each page is replete with illustrations and expressions associated with a particular letter. Encourage children to examine this book closely and invite them to list more animals and foods beginning with alphabet letters. Language arts activities, stories, chants, and shopping lists grow naturally from a chapter of soup stories and alphabet books.

Focus Book

Alphabet Soup: A Feast of Letters, by Scott Gustafson. Calico Books, 1990.

Otto moves into a new house and decides to have a housewarming party, to which he invites his friends. He asks each to bring either ingredients for soup or just an enjoyable food. The first party guest is an armadillo that brings asparagus, and the last is a zebra that brings zucchini. This A-to-Z book is replete with alliterative expressions and detailed illustrations. In the end, a fun time is had by all, especially Otto, who cooks up the soup, and makes his old friends feel at home in his new home.

Focus Book Activities

Spoken Expression

Act out the story with children taking the parts of the 26 dinner guests who bring food for the soup. Children may simply mime the parts or else announce who they are and what they will add to the soup.

Written Expression

Otto writes out a party invitation to send to his friends. Have children make soup-party invitations of another kind for this event. Would the invitation be shaped like a soup pot, or would it be in the form of a letter? Make a display of these letters and invitations.

Written Expression

Alphabet books are always popular. Have children make a display of other alphabet books. Make a class bibliography of these titles.

Written Expression

Make a shopping list of foods from A to Z that would make up a good soup. Make a shopping list of silly foods that would make up a silly alphabet soup.

Written Expression

Mix up the letters of the animals' names and the letters of the soup ingredients. Try to unscramble these for a fun word activity.

Written Expression

Have children list 26 more animals, one for each letter of the alphabet. Have them come up with even more foods for each letter. This will make children really stretch their food vocabularies.

Spoken Expression

Play alphabet games that are based on "I Unpacked Grandmother's Trunk." *Mudluscious: Stories and Activities Featuring Food for Preschool Children* has several versions, including "Alphabet Animal Soup."

Spoken Expression

Have children think of foods and activities that begin with the first letters of their names. For example, Adam ate an apple, and Bob bakes brownies. For a shorter version, have children think of just one food word or descriptive word each. For example, Josh—jelly or jumping. This is a good class introduction. Kids can add gestures to make this lively.

Longer Read Aloud Book

Burch, Robert. *Ida Early Comes Over the Mountain.* Penguin, 1980. 145 pages.

The Sutton children need a substitute mother, but Ida Early is not what they had in mind. Especially funny is the chapter called "Stew-Making Fool." This story is set in a backwoods region during the Depression.

Related Titles

Arnosky, Jim. *Raccoons and Ripe Corn.* Morrow, 1987.

Easy text and clear drawings show a family of raccoons invading a cornfield in the fall.

Banks, Kate. *Alphabet Soup.* Illustrated by Peter Sis. Knopf, 1988.

A boy plays with his alphabet soup and spells out words with the letters; each word comes alive and leads him on a magical adventure.

Brenner, Barbara. *Beef Stew.* Illustrated by Catherine Siracusa. Random House, 1990.

This beginning reader from the Step Into Reading series shows the preparation of beef stew and a friend who is invited to enjoy it with the family.

Cole, Joanna. *Who Put the Pepper in the Pot?* Illustrated by R.W. Alley. Parents Magazine Press, 1989.

The stews needs a pinch of pepper. First, no one adds it; then, everyone does! What a stew to serve to a guest.

Ehlert, Lois. *Eating the Alphabet.* Harcourt Brace Jovanovich, 1989.

"Apple to zucchini, come take a look. Start eating your way through this alphabet book." In watercolors, this book shows at least one fruit or vegetable for each letter of the alphabet. At the end are complete descriptions of each food item shown.

Ehlert, Lois. *Growing Vegetable Soup.* Harcourt Brace Jovanovich, 1987.

Solid blocks of color and large text tell the story of growing vegetables from seeds to soup.

Everitt, Betsy. *Mean Soup.* Harcourt Brace Jovanovich, 1992.

Horace, a young boy, had a bad day at school, so his mother suggests they make soup. The mother begins with water. She screams into the pot, and invites Horace to do the same. As the water boils, mother and son add dragon breath and other frustrations. A mean soup is created to stir away a bad day.

Gomi, Taro. *Who Ate It?* Millbrook, 1991.

To each question "Who ate ...?" (a particular food), the answer is shown in an illustration of an animal, or group of animals, incorporating that food's shape or color. This simple text is good as an introduction to visual clues and as a springboard for creative writing.

Haddon, Mark. *Toni and the Tomato Soup.* Harcourt Brace Jovanovich, 1988.

Tomato soup is the only thing that Toni, a fussy eater, likes to eat. But when a genie grants her a wish, Toni discovers too much of a good thing can become a nightmare. Toni's world is filled with tomato soup until she awakens and realizes it was all a dream. Or was it?

McMillan, Bruce. *Eating Fractions.* Scholastic, 1991.

Clear photographs show pizza, corn, oranges, and other foods in a variety of fractions. The pizza, for example, is cut into fourths. Pairs of pictures show a food whole and then cut. All the foods are eaten and enjoyed.

Modesitt, Jeanne. *Vegetable Soup.* Illustrated by Robin Spowart. Aladdin, 1991.

When Theodore and Elsie Rabbit discover their carrot sack is empty, they visit a variety of woodland neighbors who give them other vegetables for dinner. Although the rabbits are reluctant to eat anything they have not tried before, they make a splendid soup and invite everyone to share the feast.

Root, Phyllis. *Soup for Supper.* Illustrated by Sue Trevesdell. Harper & Row, 1986.

A wee woman plants a wonderful garden, but a giant picks all the vegetables. She tricks him by calling him names like "potato nose." (When she calls him that, he throws all the potatoes at her.) Finally, the giant admits he only wanted some soup for supper. The wee woman makes it, and they agree to share the planting and eating.

Related Activities

My Soup and My Song

The best prop for this story would be a pot of soup, to stir as you tell. Different characters can be suggested by wearing hats, shawls, jackets, and sweaters.
The story's song is sung to the tune of "Rock-a-bye Baby."

Long, long ago, in the old country, when grandmother was a girl, when days stretched out and nights came softly to tuck you in, there was a soup and there was a song.
The soup simmered gently over the fire. No one knew who first started the soup, but, as long as anyone could remember, there had always been a soup bubbling over the fire. It was made of chicken stock, rich and fragrant. Bits of this and that always went into the broth: sometimes it was a little carrot or potato, sometimes a turnip, an onion, or if it could be spared, a piece of chicken. There was always the broth to make the family feel better.

And there was the song. No one knew who first sang it, but it had been humming in the hearts of generations of this family. It was sung as the soup was made and sung as the soup was served. Sometimes it was sung with joy and sometimes with tenderness and tears.

Once the song was sung by Great-Great-Grandmother Hannah the day before her child was born.

> Simmering soup, kept warm on the hearth,
> Warm as the love that lives in my heart.
> In joy and in sorrow, laughter and tears,
> My soup and my song go on through the years.

And the child that was born to her was plump and rosy and very merry. They named her Rosa. She laughed as the soup simmered and she grew to be strong. One day, she was grown, and the soup was hers to stir. She married, but in troubled times. There was war and hunger all around. There was little bread or meat, but there was always, always the soup. And always the song. One day, soldiers came with sad news that Rosa's brother had died. That night, she seasoned the soup with her tears. And she sang the song.

> Simmering soup, kept warm on the hearth,
> Warm as the love that lives in my heart.
> In joy and in sorrow, laughter and tears,
> My soup and my song go on through the years.

A child was born to Rosa during the fighting. She was brave and she feared little. Her name was Emily. When she grew up, she carried the soup to a new land to marry a man who had already begun a new life for them. The new land was harsh, but held promise. Even after long hours of toil, the heart could be revived with the soup and with the song.

> Simmering soup, kept warm on the hearth,
> Warm as the love that lives in my heart.
> In joy and in sorrow, laughter and tears,
> My soup and my song go on through the years.

The child born to Emily, in the new land, was spirited and not easily tamed. She was as beautiful as her name, Elizabeth, but she chose to call herself Libby. She had a pioneer spirit and journeyed far. But wherever she went, she still tended the soup and sang the song.

> Simmering soup, kept warm on the hearth,
> Warm as the love that lives in my heart.
> In joy and in sorrow, laughter and tears,
> My soup and my song go on through the years.

The child born to Libby was named Anna, a gentle reminder of Libby's great-great-grandmother, Hannah. Anna grew to be strong and brave and spirited, and also very merry. She kept the soup pot simmering as all those before her had done, and on the day her daughter was born, she sang the song with gladness. She named her baby Joy, and vowed that the soup would never run out and the song would never end.

> Simmering soup, kept warm on the hearth,
> Warm as the love that lives in my heart.
> In joy and in sorrow, laughter and tears,
> My soup and my song go on through the years.

Refrigerator Raid

Characters

Bear
Pig
Cat
Lamb
Owl
Two Narrators

Stage setup: Arrange five chairs or stools in a line or semicircle; a narrator stands at each end, and the animals are seated with Bear in the middle.

Readers Theater scripts are not meant to be memorized, but read with animation. After parts are assigned, let children read over the script to get a sense of the characters they will play. For the performance, children can stand or be seated on stools. Occasionally, a character moves from one place to another (this is indicated in the script), but, in general, characters use body language to express emotions and action. For this script, characters can face away from the audience when they are outside the action.

Sing the cumulative food song to the tune of "Old MacDonald Had a Farm."

Since this story takes place at a slumber party, robes, slippers, and night caps make simple fun costumes.

Narrator 1: Bear was getting ready for his long winter's nap. But before he hibernated, he invited all his friends to a very fun slumber party.

Bear: Let's sing songs!

Pig: Let's do cheers!

Cat: Let's dance!

Lamb: I'm pooped!

Bear: Let's go to bed.

Owl: Not yet! I'm a night owl, you know.

Bear: You can stay up and read if you like, but the rest of us are ready for sleep.

Narrator 2: So they put on their pajamas and had a short pillow fight. Then everyone was ready for bed.

Bear: Goodnight, everyone.

Narrator 1: Everyone curled up in a sleeping bag, and Bear turned out the light. Ten minutes later, Bear's stomach began to growl. So he went to the kitchen.

Bear: I'm hungry as a bear. I wonder if there is anything in this refrigerator. Hey, here is a bowl of beans. I'll just heat them up in a pot for a late night snack. While I'm waiting, I'll just make up a little bean song.

Bear is hungry for a snack.
Yummy, yummy, oh.
For that snack he found some beans.
Yummy, yummy, oh.
With a bean, bean here,
And a bean, bean there,
Here a bean, there a bean,
Everywhere a bean, bean.
Bear is hungry for a snack.
Yummy, yummy, oh.

Narrator 2: All that singing woke up Pig, and he nosed his way to the kitchen.

Pig: Bear, what are you doing? All that singing woke me up.

Bear: Just having a little late night snack. Want to join me?

Pig: Sure. What are you having?

Bear: Bear is hungry for a snack.
Yummy, yummy, oh.
For that snack he found some beans.
Yummy, yummy, oh.
With a bean, bean here,
And a bean, bean there,
Here a bean, there a bean,
Everywhere a bean, bean.
Bear is hungry for a snack.
Yummy, yummy, oh.

Pig: Well, it doesn't look like there is enough for me, too. I'll just nose around in your refrigerator a bit.

Narrator 1: Pig found some parsnips. She put them in the pot with the beans, and sang a little parsnip song.

Pig: Pig is hungry for a snack.
Yummy, yummy, oh.
For that snack she found parsnips.
Yummy, yummy, oh.
With a parsnip here,
And a parsnip there,
Here a snip, there a snip,
Everywhere a parsnip.
And a bean, bean here.
And a bean, bean there.
Here a bean, there a bean,
Everywhere a bean, bean.
We are hungry for a snack.
Yummy, yummy, oh.

Narrator 2: All that singing woke up Cat.

Cat: What are you two doing? All that singing woke me up.

Bear: Just having a little late night snack. Want to join us?

Cat: Sure. What are you having?

Bear and Pig: With a bean, bean here,
And a bean, bean there,
Here a bean, there a bean,
Everywhere a bean, bean.
And a parsnip here,
And a parsnip there,
Here a snip, there a snip,
Everywhere a parsnip.
We are hungry for a snack.
Yummy, yummy, oh.

Cat: Well, it doesn't look like there is enough for me. I'll just tiptoe around in your refrigerator a bit.

Narrator 1: Cat found some corn. She put it in the pot with the beans and the parsnips, and sang a little corny song.

Cat: Cat is hungry for a snack.
Yummy, yummy, oh.
For that snack she found some corn.
Yummy, yummy, oh.
With a corn, corn here,
And a corn corn there,
Here a corn, there a corn,
Everywhere some corn, corn.
With a parsnip here,
And a parsnip there,
Here a snip, there a snip,
Everywhere a parsnip.
And a bean, bean here,
And a bean, bean there,
Here a bean, there a bean,
Everywhere a bean, bean.
We are hungry for a snack.
Yummy, yummy, oh.

Narrator 2: All that singing woke up Lamb.

Lamb: What are you guys doing? All that singing woke me up.

Bear: Just having a little late night snack. Want to join us?

Lamb: Sure. What are you having?

Bear: Beans!

Pig: Parsnips!

Cat: Corn!

Lamb: Well, it doesn't look like there is enough for me. I'll just follow you all to the refrigerator and take a peek.

Narrator 1: Lamb found some lentils. She put them in the pot with the beans and the parsnips and the corn, and sang a lovely lentil song.

Lamb: Lamb is hungry for a snack.
Yummy, yummy, oh.
For that snack she found lentils.
Yummy, yummy, oh.
With a lentil here,
And a lentil there,
Here a til, there a til,
Everywhere a lentil.
With a corn, corn here,
And a corn, corn there,
Here a corn, there a corn,
Everywhere some corn, corn.
With a parsnip here,
And a parsnip there,
Here a snip, there a snip,
Everywhere a parsnip.
And a bean bean here,
And a bean bean there,
Here a bean, there a bean,
Everywhere a bean, bean.
We are hungry for a snack.
Yummy, yummy, oh.

Narrator 2: Now, Owl was not asleep at all. She was reading. She heard all that singing, too.

Owl: How can I finish my book with all this talk of food. What are you doing?

Bear: Just having a little late night snack. Want to join us?

Owl: Sure. What are you having?

Bear: Beans!

Pig: Parsnips!

Cat: Corn!

Lamb: Lentils!

Owl: Well, it doesn't look like there is enough for me. I'll just explore this refrigerator.

Narrator 1: Owl found some onions. She put them in the pot with the other things, and sang a teary onion song.

Owl: Owl is hungry for a snack.
Yummy, yummy, oh.
For that snack she found onions.
Yummy, yummy, oh.
With an onion here,
And an onion there,
Here a yun, there a yun,
Everywhere an onion.
With a lentil here,
And a lentil there,
Here a til, there a til,
Everywhere a lentil.
With a corn, corn here,
And a corn, corn there,
Here a corn, there a corn,
Everywhere some corn corn.
With a parsnip here,
And a parsnip there,
Here a snip, there a snip,
Everywhere a parsnip.
And a bean, bean here,
And a bean, bean there,
Here a bean, there a bean,
Everywhere a bean, bean.
We are hungry for a snack.
Yummy, yummy, oh.

Narrator 2: By the time they were finished singing, they all were starved.

Narrator 1: Bear looked into the pot.

Owl: What have we got?

Bear: I think we have a big pot of bean-parsnip-corn-lentil-onion soup! Get the bowls!

Narrator 2: So the friends slurped up every spoonful.

Bear: Good friends like you are welcome to raid my refrigerator anytime. Now I'm ready for my long winter's nap.

Owl: I'm ready for bed, too.

Bear: At last. Good night, Owl. Good night, everyone. (Turn to address the audience.) And goodnight to you, too.

Other Activities

Mystery-Alphabet-Soup Word Activity

Children will learn how to make words by arranging and rearranging letters of the alphabet. This is not an easy skill, especially for children who have difficulty reading. Most children find it fun to make words out of scrambled letters. This word game reinforces decoding skills and builds vocabularies.

Prepare sets of index cards. Each card has a different letter on it. The letters for each set are placed in a sealing plastic sandwich bag or an envelope. Each set, when arranged in the right order, is the name for a different kind of soup. Here is a soup starter list:

corn	egg drop
split pea	onion
mushroom	broccoli
gumbo	cheese
minestrone	tomato
chicken	turtle
vegetable	chowder
lentil	bean
potato	

Give Me a S-O-U-P Shout!

Kids and cooks like to stir and shout about soup. Making it is fun. Making up songs, chants, and games about soup is just as enjoyable. This chant is called a "shout" because kids will want to call it out as they call out a cheer at a sports event. It is a good follow-up activity to reading many of the books in the Related Titles of this chapter (especially the zesty picture book *Mean Soup*). This chant is a call-and-response litany, beginning with the leader.

Give me a S
S
Give me an O
O
Give me a U
U
Give me a P
P

(Kids call out a kind of soup.)

Bean! (Tomato!, Chicken!, and so on.)

The leader then repeats the kind of soup and returns to the line "What? What have you got? What soup have you got?"

For a satisfying ending, the leader says; "Soup! Hot! Good in the pot!" (Stir imaginary soup and pat tummy!)

Camp Stew

Many kids have been to camp and made stew over a campfire. While cooking stew outdoors, make up a story. One kind of story is based on the "that's good/that's bad" pattern.

This group writing activity will help kids practice cause-and-effect reasoning, sequencing, and predicting outcomes. Give each group of children a large sheet of paper or poster board, and two colors of markers. At the top of the page, in one color of marker, have the children write this line: "Last week I got to go to camp." Below this line, in the other color, have them write: "That's good." The two colors will differentiate two voices in this story. Each group continues writing this story, alternating responses in this fashion:

Last week I got to go to camp.
That's good.
No, that's bad. It rained all week.
That's bad.
No, that's good. We made camp stew in the fireplace, inside.
That's good.
No, that's bad. We had to peel lots of potatoes.
That's bad.
No, that's good. We peeled all those potatoes in one hour. It was a new camp record.
That's good.
No, that's bad. Then we had to peel carrots.
That's bad.
No, that's good. Kids who peeled carrots did not have to clean their cabins.
That's good.
No, that's bad. We got locked out of the cabin and we had to spend all night in the
    kitchen, sleeping on the floor.
That's bad.
No, that's good. We were first in line for breakfast!

Rainbow Stew

If some of these vegetables are unfamiliar to the children, read the *Growing Vegetable Soup* by Ehlert. Show them the colorful pictures.

Stand in a large circle to represent the "stew pot." Say this chant as everyone marches around the circle. Children move into the center when their clothes are the color of the food mentioned. For example, when green beans are put in the pot, any child wearing green moves into the circle. Once children are inside the circle, they stay there.

Rainbow Stew, Rainbow Stew,
Try a spoonful, maybe two!
Rainbow Stew, Rainbow Stew,
What goes into Rainbow Stew?

Put in green beans.
Put in green beans.
Put in green beans.
Put them in the pot!

Put in red beets.
Put in red beets.
Put in red beets.
Put them in the pot!

Continue creating colorful vegetable verses until everyone is in the pot. Then stir—everyone turns around and around until they are ready to sit down.

Starter Kit

The "Out of the Soup Pot" Starter Kit will provide a visual aid that will introduce your food theme or unit quickly. No one can resist wondering what is inside a bag or basket so just setting it on a display or holding it up will attract attention. The items inside the container will introduce the "flavor" of the food theme and start imaginations racing. In addition, many of the items will be used in specific activities or stories, so it is easy for you to assemble. It's all in the bag!

For this chapter's theme of soup, stew and leftovers, you might pack these items into a large soup pot, stock pot, or slow cooker:

alphabet macaroni
cassette tape of "Rock-a-Bye Baby" to set the mood for the story "My Soup and My
    Song"
copy of the focus book *Alphabet Soup: A Feast of Letters*
recipes for simple soups and stews made from canned goods
canned soups and packets of dry soup mix
soup bowls, spoons, and ladles
copy of the script "Refrigerator Raid"
transparency of "Give Me a S-O-U-P Shout!"

Also for this theme, in different-size plastic storage containers (from fancy lid-popping ones to old butter tubs), place the card sets for the activity "Mystery-Alphabet-Soup Word."

Recipes

Chicken-Corn-Cheese Chowder

This "four—C" recipe is a four-star winner. First, many of the ingredients may already be on the shelf or in the freezer at home. Second, it does not take long to make, so invite a crowd for dinner at the last minute. Third, it is easy. Fourth, it is so yummy everyone will want more!

INGREDIENTS:

1 LARGE CHICKEN BREAST
1 CUP CANNED CARROTS
2 CUPS MILK
4 OUNCES (or 1 CUP) GRATED AMERICAN CHEESE
1 SMALL CAN CORN
1 CAN CREAM of POTATO SOUP
1 TEASPOON CHICKEN BOUILLON GRANULES
SALT and PEPPER to TASTE

METHOD:

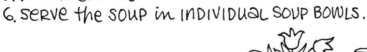

CHICKEN-CORN-CHEESE CHOWDER

1. PLACE CHICKEN BREAST IN A MICROWAVE-SAFE DISH, COVER WITH PLASTIC WRAP, and COOK 10-12 MINUTES OR UNTIL IT IS NO LONGER PINK IN THE MIDDLE. COOL CHICKEN ENOUGH TO HANDLE IT.
2. CUT THE COOLED CHICKEN BREAST INTO CHUNKS.
3. MIX UP ALL INGREDIENTS IN A BIG-POT. STIR GENTLY UNTIL EVERYTHING IS BLENDED and THE CHEESE IS MELTED THROUGHOUT.
4. COOK OVER LOW TO MEDIUM HEAT ON STOVE FOR ABOUT 30 MINUTES.
5. WATCH CLOSELY SO IT DOES NOT BURN.
6. SERVE THE SOUP IN INDIVIDUAL SOUP BOWLS.

Raid-the-Refrigerator Stew

In the script "Refrigerator Raid," the animals make a soup from leftover food they find when raiding the refrigerator. This inspires kids to raid their own refrigerators and shelves and concoct stews. This recipe is designed to teach one method of making stew. Encourage kids to create their own variations.

INGREDIENTS:

1½ POUNDS MEAT (BEEF, PORK, LAMB, VEAL, and SO on)
1 CAN BROTH (BEEF or CHICKEN) or CREAM of CELERY SOUP
1 PACKAGE DRY SOUP MIX (ONION or OTHER)
1 TEASPOON MUSTARD or ¼ CUP KETCHUP
½ TEASPOON THYME or 1 TABLESPOON PARSLEY FLAKES
4 CUPS of VEGETABLES (POTATO, CARROT, ONION, CELERY, GREEN PEPPER, and SO on)
SALT and PEPPER to TASTE

METHOD:

RAID-the-REFRIGERATOR STEW

1. CUT the MEAT into 1-INCH CUBES.
2. PUT DRY SOUP MIX into a PLASTIC BAG or a BROWN BAG and ADD the MEAT, a LITTLE at a TIME, TOSSING the MEAT SO it GETS COATED with the SOUP MIX.
3. SET the MEAT ASIDE.
4. WASH, PEEL, and CUT the VEGETABLES into CHUNKS.
5. IN a BOWL, MIX the MUSTARD with the BROTH (or the KETCHUP with the CREAM of CELERY SOUP) UNTIL BLENDED.
6. PUT the MEAT into the BOTTOM of an OVEN-SAFE POT, and PUT the VEGETABLES on TOP of the MEAT.
7. POUR or SPOON the BROTH-MUSTARD (or SOUP-KETCHUP) MIXTURE on TOP.
8. SPRINKLE the HERBS (THYME or PARSLEY) on TOP.
9. COVER the POT and BAKE it in a 350-DEGREE OVEN for 1½ HOURS.
10. AS IT IS COOKING, OCCASIONALLY CHECK and STIR the STEW. IF IT SEEMS DRY, ADD a LITTLE BROTH, WATER, or MILK, and STIR.

Chapter 8

Out of the World's Breadbasket

Introduction

Interest in ethnic restaurants and diverse food has grown in the past decade. Much of this is reflected by the growth of multicultural books published in the United States. Food preferences may be culturally specific, but here is an opportunity to explore these differences and to learn to try new food. To appreciate differences in food may be a first step in appreciating differences among people and their customs.

Food does more than fill the stomach. It is central to many religious and deeply held beliefs. For example, the Jewish Seder, the main service of Passover, takes place at a family table. Each food served has symbolic significance. Bitter herbs dipped in salt water symbolize the tears Jewish people shed during the bitter time of their slavery in Egypt over 3000 years ago. Another example, the southeastern American Indian tribes mark the growth of new corn and a new year with the Green Corn ceremony.

Food is a focus of holidays around the world. Mexican fried pastry (bunuelos) is served on cracked pottery dishes on Christmas Eve. Traditionally, the dishes are then thrown to the ground, signifying the end of the old year and the beginning of the new. Each food in an African-American Kwanzaa holiday has special meaning. One ear of corn for each child in the family is put on a special place mat.

American middle-class children may have little understanding about food in other cultures. For example, while fat and oil may mean health and prosperity in developing nations, they are seen as a cause of high cholesterol and heart disease in the United States. This chapter presents opportunities for children to have direct experiences with other cultures. Many children, already familiar with tacos, spaghetti, pizza, and egg rolls, can be encouraged to explore new tastes. Consult the ethnic cookbooks in the Resource Bibliography and try dishes that are less common.

A number of this chapter's picture books are set in eastern Europe and describe Jewish food. Hanukkah stories featuring latkes are the most common. *Malke's Secret Recipe* and *Latkes and Applesauce* are two recent titles about these potato pancakes. Native American, Hispanic, and African stories include the Nigerian legend *Why the Sky Is Far Away*, and *Dragonfly's Tale*, a legend adapted from the Zuni people. *Family Pictures* describes everyday activities, many of which involve cooking and eating food.

Everybody Cooks Rice was chosen as the focus book for this chapter because of its international understanding and its universal theme. Set in a multiethnic neighborhood, two children visit neighbors from Barbados, Puerto Rico, Vietnam, and Haiti. In each home, rice is served in a different, delicious way. Enrichment activities inspired by this book include writing international menus and planning a neighborhood potluck.

Social studies units on any country can be enhanced with a food component. Geography and history come to life when they are experienced through food. New words in new languages, creative art projects, and folk music all incite children to sample a culture as well as its foods.

Focus Book

Everybody Cooks Rice, by Norah Dooley. Illustrations by Peter J. Thornton. Carolrhoda, 1991

Mother sends Carrie out to find her younger brother, Andrew, and bring him home for dinner. As Carrie looks for him, she discovers everyone in their multiethnic neighborhood is cooking rice, in a variety of ways, for dinner. The range includes black-eyed peas and rice from Barbados, Puerto Rican rice cooked in turmeric, Vietnamese rice with nuoc cham (a fish sauce), and creole style Haitian rice with hot peppers.

Focus Book Activities

Written Expression

Have children make an international menu for each family, complete with all the foods each family might eat alongside the rice dish.

Spoken Expression

This story is told from Carrie's point of view, with almost no dialogue. Retell the story with dialogue.

Written Expression with Bonus Activity

Rewrite this story supposing Andrew stays at the first house, with the family from Barbados. Describe the way the family lives, and what other foods they enjoy. This written activity will involve library research to learn about Barbados. This activity can be a springboard to study about all the places mentioned in the book—Barbados, Puerto Rico, Vietnam, India, China, Haiti, France, and Italy. A culminating event for this unit could be an international food fair or a cooking affair featuring the different rice dishes mentioned in this book.

Written and Spoken Expression

Make a vocabulary list of all the foods mentioned. Have each student find at least one new food dish from another culture and teach that word to the class.

Written Expression

Write another international food story in which Andrew visits the same neighborhood on a night the neighbors are having desserts, or vegetables, noodle dishes, or whatever.

Longer Read Aloud Book

Scieszka, Jon. *Knights of the Kitchen Table*. Penguin, 1991. 55 pages.

The adventures of the Time Warp Trio, around the world and out of this world. This time, they begin at the kitchen table and end up in King Arthur's Court.

Related Titles

Adler, David. *Malke's Secret Recipe*. Illustrated by Jan Halpern. Kar-Ben Copies, 1989.

In a little Jewish town, Malke makes the best latkes (potato pancakes), but she will not share her recipe. One day, a neighbor watches on secretly as Malke makes them, and he plans to make some of his own. As he prepares the pancakes, his wife watches on and makes changes in the recipe. For example, he wrote down that Malke put in a few drops of lemon juice, but his wife scoffs that lemon is for tea, not latkes. The end result? The neighbors' latkes do not taste at all like Malke's.

Ashley, Bernard. *Cleversticks*. Illustrated by Derek Brazell. Crown, 1991.

Ling Sung is not as skillful as his school classmates at many tasks. The other children discover he is adept in using chopsticks, though.

Bruchac, Joseph. *The First Strawberries: A Cherokee Story*. Illustrated by Anna Vojtech. Dial, 1993.

This Cherokee tale about the origin of strawberries tells how the sun magically makes these berries to teach the lesson of forgiveness to an angry woman who seems determined to leave her husband because of his coldness. The tale, like the strawberries, reminds us "that friendship and respect are as sweet as the taste of ripe, red berries."

Buchanan, Joan. *Nothing But Yams for Supper*. Illustrated by Jirina Morton. Firefly Books. 1988.

Alice travels to different countries to find a place to have yams for supper. All the other countries point out their special foods, and she tries some. She likes the ones that are as "soft and mushy and yummy" as yams.

Choi, Sook Nyul. *Halmoni and the Picnic*. Illustrated by Karen M. Dugan. Houghton Mifflin, 1993.

When Yunmi's grandmother comes to America from Korea, Yunmi invites her to a school picnic. Yunmi worries that Halmoni (the grandmother) will be laughed at because of her food and clothing. Instead, the children enjoy meeting her, and Halmoni begins to like America.

Czernecki, Stefan. *The Sleeping Bread*. Hyperion, 1992.

Beto owns a bakery shop in the village of San Pedro, Guatemala, and he feeds Zafiro, a beggar who is avoided by most people in the village. When Zafiro decides to leave, he sheds a tear into the baker's water jug, and, overnight, the bread stops rising. Everyone tries to help, but only when the beggar returns and washes away the tears does Beto's bread rise again. Brilliantly colored folk art designs make the book a visual treat.

dePaola, Tomie. *Jamie O'Rourke and the Big Potato*. Putnam, 1992.

The laziest man in Ireland is Jamie O'Rourke. But he is a lucky man, too, and he traps a leprechaun who grants him a wish. Jamie wishes for all the potatoes he can eat, but that wish proves to be more than he can stomach!

dePaola, Tomie. *Tony's Bread.* Putnam, 1989.

This fanciful book traces the origin of "poettone," a sweet, Italian bread. Tony is a baker with one daughter. Though she is old enough to marry, Tony does not allow her father to even speak to an eligible man. Then one day, rich Angelo comes to town and falls in love with the bread and the daughter. Angelo's plot to marry the daughter brings good fortune to Tony and fame to his bread.

Drucker, Malka. *Grandma's Latkes.* Harcourt Brace Jovanovich, 1992

The year Molly is old enough to help Grandma prepare latkes for Hanukkah, she learns the story of the festival, as well as Grandma's secret recipe. Her latke recipe is included in the book.

Garza, Carman Lomas. *Family Pictures. Cuadrosde Familia.* Children's Book Press, 1990.

English and Spanish texts describe "snapshots" of the family involved in various activities throughout the year, many of which include preparing food or eating. There are dishes from rabbit to watermelon, and a good picture and description of a "cake walk."

Gerson, Mary-Joan. *Why the Sky Is Far Away.* Illustrated by Carla Golembe. Little, Brown, 1992.

In the beginning, the sky was close enough to the earth that people could cut off chunks of it to eat. The sky grew angry when the people began to waste it, so it moved far away. After that, people had to till land and plant crops. Mixed media art adds to the appeal of this Nigerian folk tale.

Greene, Ellin. *The Legend of the Cranberry.* Illustrated by Brad Sneed. Simon and Schuster, 1993.

In this retelling of a Delaware Indian legend, Great Spirit gives cranberries to the world to remind people of the great battle between the native people and the mastodon.

Hillman, Elizabeth. *Min-Yo and the Moon Dragon.* Illustrated by John Wallner. Harcourt Brace Jovanovich, 1992.

Long ago, when the moon seemed to be moving too close to the earth, the emperor of China sent the smallest girl on earth to seek out the moon dragon for assistance. Min-Yo, the resourceful girl, feeds the dragon, and together they discover a way to stop the moon's fall.

Levine, Arthur A. *Pearl Moscowitz's Last Stand.* Illustrated by Robert Roth. William Morrow, 1993.

In an ethnically changing neighborhood, Pearl Moscowitz grew up. Her mother helped plant flowering trees on her street. As the neighborhood changes, new groups introduce new food to share, and all watch the destruction of the beautiful trees. Finally, Pearl has had enough and she makes an international last stand.

Manushkin, Fran. *Latkes and Applesauce.* Illustrated by Robin Spowart. Scholastic, 1990.

Long ago, a blizzard covered the apples and potatoes that were to be used to make applesauce and latkes for the Menasch family's Hanukkah feast. They made do with soup, and took in a lost cat and a lost dog during the storm. At the end of eight days, the sky cleared. The dog dug up the potatoes, thus giving him his new name. The cat found the apples, miraculously still left on the apple tree, thus giving her a name, too. This brought about once more the miracle of the Hanukkah feast, in the true spirit of the holiday.

Morgan, Pierr. *The Turnip*. Philomel, 1990.

This version of the old Russian tale is particularly popular with storytellers because of its rhythm and its rhyme. Dedouska plants a turnip seed that grows into a turnip so large that he cannot pull it up. His wife Baboushka comes to help, and then so do Mashenka the granddaughter, Geouchka the dog, and Keska the cat. With the help of everyone, including a little field mouse, the giant turnip comes up. A final illustration shows it cooking in a large pot.

Morris, Ann. *Bread Bread Bread*. Photographs by Ken Heyman. William Morrow, 1989.

Clear photographs show bread from all over the world, and the people who make and eat it.

Peters, Russell M. *Clambake—a Wampanoag Tradition*. Lerner, 1992.

This longer picture book, one in a native American series, tells the story of a 12-year-old Wampanoag Indian boy in Massachusetts who learns to prepare for an appanaug, or clambake, from his grandfather.

Polacco, Patricia. *Rechenka's Eggs*. Philomel, 1988.

Babushka, an old woman, rescues an injured goose that accidentally breaks her carefully decorated eggs. The goose lays 13 miraculous eggs, each with colored designs, to replace the broken ones. Babushka takes these to the Easter Festival in Maocva, where they win first prize. The goose, Rechenka, is gone when Babuska returns home. One last egg hatches into a goose that stays with her. In addition to the decorated eggs, Palacco includes other authentic Ukrainian foods in this story, such as kuluch, a sweet bread spread with pashka—a spread of cheese, butter, and raisins.

Polacco, Patricia. *Thunder Cake*. Putnam, 1990.

The young girl is frightened of the coming storm until her grandmother teaches her to make Thunder Cake. As they gather the ingredients and mix the cake, the girl forgets the storm. When the thunder cracks overhead, they are eating the first piece.

Rattigan, Jama Kim. *Dumpling Soup*. Illustrated by Lillian Hsu-Flanders. Little, Brown, 1993.

Set in Hawaii, this story of a young Asian-American girl's efforts to make dumplings for the New Year's dumpling soup was a winner in the publisher's New Voices, New World contest, which encourages writers from diverse racial backgrounds.

Regguinti, Gordon. *The Sacred Harvest: Ojibway Wild Rice Gathering*. Lerner, 1992.

This longer picture book tells the story of an 11-year-old Ojibway boy's first experience, alongside his father, gathering and processing mahnomin, or wild rice, a sacred food of their people.

Rodanas, Kristina. *Dragonfly's Tale*. Clarion, 1992.

In this story adapted from a Zuni tale, two children regain the Corn Maiden's blessing after a poor harvest. The children's kindness and prudent behavior teach the Zuni people to not take the Corn Maiden's gifts for granted so they will be blessed with rich harvests of corn in the future.

San Souci, Robert. *The Talking Eggs*. Illustrated by Jerry Pinkney. Dial, 1988.

In this Creole folk tale, a sweet girl, Blanche, shows kindness to an old witch and is rewarded with a pot of stew and with talking eggs that bring her great riches. Her selfish mother and spoiled favored sister try to find these treasures, but they never succeed.

Soto, Gary. *Too Many Tamales*. Illustrated by Ed Martinez. Putnam, 1993.

Marie helps her mother make tamales for the Christmas dinner. When her mother leaves the kitchen, Maria tries on her mother's diamond ring. Later, the ring is thought to be lost in the tamales. Maria and her cousins eat the tamales, but the ring turns up in a surprise ending.

Related Activities

The Secret Recipe of the Lotsapasta Family

It will help children who are unfamiliar with Italian cooking to have samples of each spice to smell before beginning the story.

Teach the children to say "Delici-o-so!" on cue in the story, and lead them in the participation indicated.

The Lotsapasta family liked spaghetti with a delicious sauce that was a secret family recipe. They liked the sauce to have onion and garlic and oregano and basil. It was a very special sauce.

One day, Mama Lotsapasta put a pot of spaghetti sauce on the stove. Soon it began to simmer, and the smell was, as Mama said, "Delici-o-so!" Mama Lotsapasta lifted the lid off the pot and put in a long wooden spoon. She stirred the pot (pretend to stir) and took out a spoonful. Mama Lotsapasta blew on the sauce to cool it, and then she tasted it (slurp!). "Delici-o-so!" But it needed a little more ...

"Onion," said Mama Lotsapasta. She added another cup of chopped onion and put the lid back on the pot. Then Mama Lotsapasta went out to weed the garden.

Before long, the nose of Papa Lotsapasta began to catch the wonderful smell coming from the kitchen. He did not see Mama Lotsapasta anywhere so he lifted the lid and put in a long wooden spoon. He stirred the pot (pretend to stir) and took out a spoonful. Papa Lotsapasta blew on the sauce to cool it and then tasted it (slurp!). "Delici-o-so!" But it needed a little more ...

"Garlic! This sauce needs more garlic," said Papa Lotsapasta. So he added another clove of garlic and put the lid back on the pot. Then Papa Lotsapasta went to fold the laundry.

Soon the school bus arrived and little Leonardo Lotsapasta came into the kitchen. He could see that the lid on the pot of sauce almost danced as the sauce simmered. He did not see Mama Lotsapasta anywhere, so he lifted the lid and put in a long wooden spoon. He stirred the pot (pretend to stir) and took out a spoonful. Little Leonardo Lotsapasta blew on the sauce to cool it and then tasted it (slurp!). "Delici-o-so!" But it needed a little more ...

"Oregano! This sauce needs more Oregano," said little Leonardo Lotsapasta. So he added a dash more oregano—well, really more like four dashes—and put the lid back on the pot. Then little Leonardo Lotsapasta went to do his homework.

Then lovely Lucinda Lotsapasta came home. Even outside she could hear the bubbling of the sauce as it simmered. She did not see Mama Lotsapasta anywhere, so she lifted the lid and put in a long wooden spoon. She stirred the pot (pretend to stir) and took out a spoonful. Lovely Lucinda Lotsapasta blew on the sauce to cool it and then tasted it (slurp!). "Delici-o-so!" But it needed a little more ...

"Basil! This sauce needs more basil," said lovely Lucinda Lotsapasta. So she added a pinch more basil—well, really more like two pinches—and put the lid back on the pot. Then lovely Lucinda Lotsapasta went to deliver newspapers on her route.

Soon the family gathered at the dinner table. Mama brought out a tossed salad. Papa brought out garlic bread. Little Leonardo brought out Parmesan cheese, and lovely Lucinda carried out a big bowl of spaghetti. The family all watched and sniffed as Mama uncovered the sauce. Then they all helped themselves and began to eat.

Mama said, "Delici-o-so! I'm glad I put in extra onion. That's what makes this sauce so special."

Papa said, "You what? I put in extra garlic. That's what makes this sauce so special."

Little Leonardo said, "Not! I put in extra oregano. That's what makes this sauce so special."

Lovely Lucinda said, "Don't be silly. I put in extra basil. That's what makes this sauce so special."

So they all took another bite, and another, and another, as they argued about which spice made the sauce so special. Soon the sauce was almost gone, but still they could not decide. Just at that moment, Grandpa Lotsapasta returned from the bakery. He piled the last of the spaghetti and sauce onto his plate. He took one bite.

"Ah," he said. "Plenty of onion."

He took a second bite. "Ah," he said. "Plenty of garlic."

He took a third bite. "Ah," he said. "Plenty of oregano."

He cleaned his plate. "Ah," he said. "Plenty of basil."

The Lotsapastas looked at each other and started to laugh. "So," said Mama Lotsapasta. "That is the secret to a very special sauce. Put in lots of EVERYTHING!" And from that day on, that is just what they did.

Plenty to Go Around

Characters

Lion
Elephant
Monkey
Rabbit
Cobra
Two Narrators

Background: The setting for this story is eastern Africa, and the dinner described is similar to an Ethiopian meal. Guests are seated at a table covered with an Injera, a sourdough, pancake-like bread. Food is brought to the table and served directly onto this edible tablecloth. Guests tear off small portions of the Injera to scoop up the food. When all the food is consumed, the Injera is then eaten.

Describe this experience before the story is performed so children will understand the importance of the Injera.

Stage setup: Arrange five chairs or stools in a line or semicircle; a narrator stands at each far edge of the stage area.

Readers Theater scripts are not meant to be memorized, but read with animation. After parts are assigned, let children read over the script to get a sense of the characters they will play. For the performance, children can stand or be seated on stools. Occasionally, a character moves from one place to another (this is indicated in the script), but, in general, characters use body language to express emotions and action. For this script, when Cobra, Monkey, and Rabbit disappear from the table setting, the characters get off their stools and turn their backs to the audience.

Prepare face masks for the characters of Lion, Elephant, Monkey, Rabbit, and Cobra using the patterns on pages 120-21.

ENLARGE 3-4X
to FIT CHILDREN'S
FACES. MASKS
COULD BE GLUED
to PAPER PLATES.

Narrator 1: In a part of eastern Africa, times had been hard, and there wasn't all that much food to eat. Still, Lion wanted to have a banquet. He prepared an Injera, a special pancake to cover the table, and on this edible tablecloth the food would be served.

Narrator 2: Next, he invited all his friends. Because there really was very little food, as each guest arrived, Lion said—

Lion: Please don't take more than your share. Then there will be plenty to go around.

Narrator 1: Elephant arrived first.

Elephant: I am so hungry I could eat everything on the table and the Injera, too.

Lion: Please don't take more than your share. Then there will be plenty to go around.

Elephant: Of course. Just give me a little of that chicken stew.

Narrator 2: Monkey arrived next.

Monkey: I am so hungry I could eat everything on the table and the Injera, too.

Lion: Please don't take more than your share. Then there will be plenty to go around.

Monkey: Of course. Just give me a little of that yogurt.

Narrator 1: Rabbit arrived next.

Rabbit: I am so hungry I could eat everything on the table and the Injera, too.

Lion: Please don't take more than your share. Then there will be plenty to go around.

Rabbit: Of course. Just give me a little pepper salad.

Narrator 2: Cobra came last.

Cobra: I am so hungry I could eat everything on the table and the Injera, too.

Lion: Please don't take more than your share. Then there will be plenty to go around.

Cobra: Just how big is my share? I have my own idea about that.

Narrator 1: Elephant looked at Lion. Lion looked at Elephant.

Narrator 2: Elephant said quietly to Lion—

Elephant: I don't trust Cobra. He may do something dreadful.

Lion: We will have to keep an eye on him.

Narrator 1: So the friends sat down to eat. Each took only his share, but the food was so good that they enjoyed every bite. And they forgot to watch Cobra. (Cobra gets off stool and sits behind it.)

Lion: Please excuse me while I get more water.

Narrator 2: Elephant was the first to notice that something was wrong.

Elephant: Where is Cobra, and what is that lump under the Injera?

Lion: Dear me, I thought you were going to keep an eye on him. Please excuse me while I get some lemon for Monkey's yogurt. (Monkey gets off stool and sits behind it.)

Narrator 1: While Lion was gone, Elephant noticed—

Elephant: Where is Monkey and what is that big lump under the Injera? And I still can't find Cobra.

Lion: Dear me, I thought you were going to keep an eye on Cobra. I am afraid he is up to something dreadful. Please excuse me one more time. I must get the salt and pepper for Rabbit's salad. (Rabbit gets off stool and sits behind it.)

Narrator 2: While Lion was gone, Elephant noticed—

Elephant: Something is dreadfully wrong! Where are Rabbit and Monkey and what is that huge lump under the Injera? And I still can't find Cobra.

Lion: Something is dreadfully wrong.

Elephant: I told you I didn't trust Cobra. I'll bet you he has eaten more than his share. That lump is Cobra. He probably pulled Rabbit and Monkey under the Injera and ate them!

Lion: Then, we must do something.

Elephant: I could whack him with my trunk.

Lion: No, no. That might injure Monkey and Rabbit.

Elephant: Then we'll just have to get him to come out.

Narrator 1: So Lion whispered to Elephant so Cobra wouldn't hear—

Lion: I have a plan. Let's pretend that Aardvark dropped by unexpectedly, with a big pot of beef stew.

Elephant: I get it. Then Cobra will want to come out to eat his share, and then we can save our friends.

Narrator 2: So Lion and Elephant spoke in loud voices so Cobra would be sure to hear.

Lion: Hello, Aardvark! How nice of you to stop by.

Elephant: That certainly is a good-looking beef stew you brought just as we were running out of food.

Lion: Just put it on the Injera.

Narrator 1: The plan worked. Cobra stuck his head out from under the Injera. (Cobra climbs back onto stool.)

Narrator 2: And when he did, Elephant took hold of Cobra and he pulled and he pulled and he pulled.

Lion: Keep pulling, Elephant!

Narrator 1: And out popped Monkey. (Monkey climbs back onto stool.)

Lion: Keep pulling, Elephant.

Narrator 2: Then, out popped Rabbit. (Rabbit climbs back onto stool.)

Lion: Keep pulling, Elephant! I want to have a word with Cobra.

Narrator 1: Soon, Cobra was out from under the Injera.

Lion: Oh, Cobra. I asked you to eat only your share. You should share *with* Monkey and Rabbit, not eat your share *of* Monkey and Rabbit. You are no longer welcome at my table.

Narrator 2: So Cobra slithered away. (Cobra gets off stool.)

Narrator 2: Then, Lion invited everyone else to sit back down.

Lion: Good friends, the stew, the yogurt, and the salad are nearly gone, but please join me in eating the Injera, too. When good friends take only their share, there will always be plenty to go around.

Other Activities

Native American Food Map

(Cross-Curricular Project)

This activity will encourage children to discover more about foods enjoyed by different Native American peoples. It draws upon social studies, art, and literature, so the projects become cross-cultural, as well.

Make a large mural map of the United States and have students design a map legend for the foods that have been eaten by native peoples in different parts of the country. The designs on page 126 can be used, but encourage students to create their own symbols.

The five geographical areas listed below, with sample foods and suggestions for class activities, will encourage students to discover more about food origins and customs. This will serve as an introduction to native peoples and the foods that they ate. The brief explanations of some of the more unusual foods will motivate students to research and prepare these dishes. *Spirit of the Harvest* is an excellent cookbook for the teacher or librarian.

Because food stories and rituals are central to Native American cultures, students will want to explore legends about the origins of foods among native peoples. Two picture books,

The Legend of the Cranberry and *The First Strawberries: A Cherokee Story*, listed in the bibliography of this chapter, will complement this project.

Geographical Areas, Foods, Projects

The Southeast

Choctaw, Hominy Soup

Hominy is dried corn removed from the cob, soaked in hot water, and mixed with wood ashes. The kernels puff up, and they are piled in fresh water until tender, then dried for later use. Have students sample hominy. Canned hominy is readily available in supermarkets.

Cherokee, Spiced Jerusalem Artichokes

Still a popular Indian food, the Jerusalem artichoke grows from the roots of a sunflower. The roots are dug up in the fall, and spiced or pickled. Bring in Jerusalem artichokes for students to see.

Cherokee, Persimmon Pudding

Persimmons grow wild in the southeastern United States. Canned persimmon pulp can be purchased if students wish to make this dish.

The Northeast

Ojibway, Wild Rice Johnny Cakes

The Ojibway and Menomiee tribes process wild rice as their ancestors did. This dish uses wild rice instead of cornmeal.

Cook wild rice for students to sample and make this dish. Read *The Sacred Harvest*, by Gordon Regguinti, the story of an Ojibway boy and his family's wild rice harvest.

Indian Pudding

Today, this is served as a dessert, but native peoples such as the Iroquois served it along with meat and vegetables in the late morning, as part of the main meal of the day.

Students will enjoy making Indian pudding for a class treat. It is delicious served with ice cream, and whipped cream, too.

The Great Plains

Cattail Pollen Flapjacks

Cattails were eaten at various stages of their growing seasons. The young shoots were eaten raw or in salads; the pollen or blossoms were combined with wheat flower to make flapjacks for this dish.

Bring in cattails for students to see. Examine the pollen, or simply make a display of cattails for the classroom.

The Southwest

Pueblo, Fried Squash Blossoms

Bright orange squash blossoms were used in religious ceremonies, and fried as food in Pueblo ceremonies.

Try to find squash blossoms or bring in squash for students to enjoy.

Pima-Papago, Cactus and Eggs

The Papago reservation relies on cactus for food, since the cactus can be grown where annual rainfall is as little as five inches. The barrel cactus holds a whitish liquid that can be used in this dish.

Cactus also comes canned, if students wish to prepare the dish.

The West

Shawnee, Elk Stew with Acorn Dumplings

Elk, also called "wapiti" or pale deer by the Shawnee, was used in stew and served with dumplings made from acorns or ground hazelnuts.

Students can make a close version of this from beef steak.

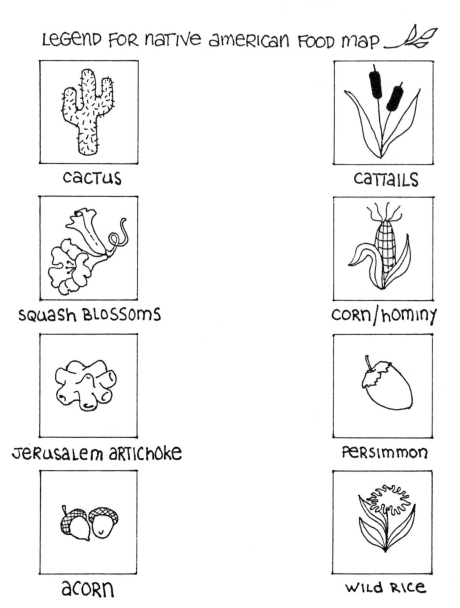

LEGEND FOR NATIVE AMERICAN FOOD MAP

cactus

cattails

squash blossoms

corn/hominy

jerusalem artichoke

persimmon

acorn

wild rice

A Family Scrapbook

Celebrating Food Around the World

A Writing and Family History Activity

This activity is inspired by Carmen Lomas Garza's "story picture" paintings in the book *Family Pictures*. Have children tell about family food customs, holiday meals, or food stories using pictures and words. Before students tell their stories, share several books about food enjoyed by families from different ethnic backgrounds. Selections might include *Family Pictures*, *Too Many Tamales*, *Latkes and Applesauce*, and *Everybody Cooks Rice*.

Collect all the pictures and stories and make a class scrapbook celebrating the diversity of story and food in a spirit of community. Family photographs of holiday meals and celebrations could be included.

Older children may wish to make this project a mixed media scrapbook by adding taped conversations with older family members about favorite family recipes and food stories. Most families have a favorite food story to share. Video tapes, slides, and old family movies could be brought to class for a longer project combining oral histories and storytelling.

World Stew

Writing and Speaking Activity

The teacher or librarian can prepare a "world stew" with students to discover food stories and food customs around the world, to encourage an understanding of ethnic diversity and a respect among people around the world.

The teacher begins this activity by bringing in a large pot and saying, "World travelers sample foods from every corner of the world. Not everyone eats alike, but we must all eat to live. Not everyone is alike, but we all must share this world if anyone is to live at all. May we each add something to our world stew in a spirit of community."

The teacher then begins the sharing with a statement such as: "I add peanuts from Kenya. Peanuts are a staple in stews and soups in many African diets. Peanut soup is enjoyed in Kenya." Peanut soup can be prepared for the class to sample, or the teacher can simply add peanuts to the pot.

Each student continues this pattern by saying, "I add _____ from _____." The student then describes the food and tells a story, or gives information about it, to the group. Encourage students to prepare the food, or bring items associated with that food, to add to the world stew.

Stir Fry Cry

Chant

Use this chant with children as a brainstorming activity to create stir fry dishes. It is both a language arts activity and a food experience. Use the two recipes for stir fry on pages 131-32 as a related activity.

Stir fry,
Stir fry,
Oh my stir fry!

I cry,
You cry,
We all cry for stir fry!

Chop up veggies,
What do we need?
(Kids suggest veggies)
Green pepper, celery,
We'll have a feed!

(Leader adds several quick rhymes)
Bean sprouts, bean sprouts,
Good and crunchy!
Add a handful,
Oh so munchy!

Soy sauce, soy sauce
Add a dash!
What else to add,
For our Chinese bash?

(Have kids suggest other foods here such as chicken, pork, beef, and ham. To keep the rhythm going, the whole group says the following verse after each food is added.)

Stir fry,
Stir fry,
Oh my stir fry!

A good ending can be:

Stir fry,
Stir fry,
We all cry for stir fry!

Round-the-World Treats

Poem

This poem introduces some of the more unusual foods found around the world. Use it in a social studies unit and have children locate the places on a world map. Have them research food and cooking for places they want to visit.

Off we fly
To sun filled Hawaii,
For pineapple, papaya
And mahi-mahi.

In Japan there's tempura
And sashimi,
The rice is hot
And always steamy.

In Istanbul
Try nuts and figs,
In Denmark
Find the finest pigs.

Having a Fine Time

After learning facts about foods from other cultures, have children make postcards about what they have learned. Each child chooses a country and decorates one side of a 3-by-5-inch card with drawings or cutouts of landmarks. A message on the back should include the kind of food they would be eating if they could really visit the country. For example, a child choosing France could draw a picture of the Eiffel Tower and write to a friend about eating crêpe, suzette. When the cards are complete, you might display them on a world map for a further geography tie-in.

Starter Kit

The "Out of the World's Breadbasket" Starter Kit will provide a visual aid that will introduce your food theme or unit quickly. No one can resist wondering what is inside a bag or basket so just setting it on a display or holding it up will attract attention. The items inside the container will introduce the "flavor" of the food theme and start imaginations racing. In addition, many of the items will be used in specific activities or stories, so it is easy for you to assemble. It's all in the bag!

For this international food theme, you might pack these items into a large breadbasket covered with a bright cloth:

small containers of onion, garlic, oregano, and basil to smell with the story "The Secret Recipe of the Lotsapasta Family"
breads from different cultures such as pita bread, rice cakes, tortillas, French bread, matzo, and challah (Jewish holiday bread)

copy of the focus book *Everybody Cooks Rice*
world map or globe
map of the United States with native American traditional territories marked
fortune cookies, for a treat
pasta maker, garlic press, wok, chopsticks
ingredients to make ethnic foods such as rice noodles, salsa, tahini (sesame seed paste)
copies of the recipe pages for each child
copy of the script "Plenty to Go Around"
transparency of the chant "Stir Fry Cry"

Recipes

Sweet-and-Sour Stir Fry

This sweet-and-sour recipe can be made with or without meat. If hesitant about kids cooking with hot oil, have an adult do this part, and let the kids mix the sauce and add it to the already-cooked meat and veggies.

INGREDIENTS

MEAT STIR FRY
- 2 CUPS MEAT
- 1 TABLESPOON SOY SAUCE
- 1 TABLESPOON WATER
- 2 TABLESPOONS CORNSTARCH
- ½ CUP COOKING OIL
- ½ GREEN PEPPER, CUT IN CHUNKS
- 2 CARROTS, CUT IN CHUNKS
- ½ CUP ONION, CUT IN CHUNKS
- 1 CLOVE GARLIC
- 1 CUP CANNED PINEAPPLE CHUNKS

VEGGIE STIR FRY
- 1 GREEN PEPPER, CUT IN CHUNKS
- 2 CARROTS, CUT IN CHUNKS
- 2 STALKS CELERY, CUT IN CHUNKS
- ½ CUP ONION, CUT IN CHUNKS
- 2 CUPS CAULIFLOWER, CUT IN CHUNKS
- 1 CUP CANNED PINEAPPLE
- ½ CUP COOKING OIL

SAUCE
- ⅔ CUP SUGAR
- ¼ CUP CATSUP
- ⅓ CUP PINEAPPLE JUICE from canned pineapple
- ½ CUP CIDER VINEGAR
- 2 TABLESPOONS SOY SAUCE
- 2 TABLESPOONS CORNSTARCH mixed with ½ CUP WATER

METHOD:

MEAT STIR FRY
(WITH VEGGIES ADDED)

1. IN A BOWL, STIR MEAT INTO THE SOY SAUCE, WATER, AND CORNSTARCH. FRY MEAT IN OIL UNTIL BROWN. ADD ONION, GREEN PEPPER, AND CARROTS. FRY ABOUT 2 MINUTES MORE. SET ASIDE.

2. MIX SAUCE INGREDIENTS TOGETHER AND ADD TO THE FRIED MEAT-VEGGIE MIXTURE. COOK AGAIN UNTIL SAUCE THICKENS. ADD PINEAPPLE CHUNKS AND SERVE.

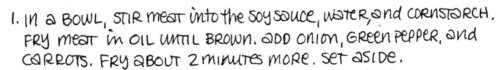

VEGGIE VERSION

1. STIR FRY ALL THE VEGGIES IN OIL FOR ABOUT 2 MINUTES.

2. MIX SAUCE AND ADD TO VEGGIES. COOK AGAIN UNTIL SAUCE THICKENS. ADD PINEAPPLE CHUNKS AND SERVE.

Basic Chicken Stir Fry

INGREDIENTS:

½ POUND MUSHROOMS, SLICED
½ CUP GREEN ONIONS, CHOPPED
½ POUND NUTS
2 TABLESPOONS OIL
½ CUP each of as many of
   the OPTIONS as you LIKE
1 CUP BOILING WATER

2 CHICKEN BOUILLON CUBES
⅓ CUP SOY sauce
1 TEASPOON GROUND GINGER
2 TABLESPOONS CORNSTARCH
1 POUND CHICKEN, CUT into
   CUBES

METHOD:

BASIC CHICKEN STIR FRY

1. FRY CHICKEN in OIL in a FRYING PAN UNTIL LIGHTLY BROWN. ADD MUSHROOMS, ONIONS, and NUTS, and COOK another minute. ADD any of the OPTIONAL INGREDIENTS and COOK another 1-2 minutes. SET aside.

2. MIX the BOUILLON, BOILING WATER, SOY SAUCE, GINGER, and CORN-STARCH TOGETHER UNTIL DISSOLVED. POUR THIS OVER the CHICKEN and OTHER INGREDIENTS in the PAN.

3. COOK JUST UNTIL SAUCE THICKENS.

4. SERVE THIS WITH HOT RICE.

A Jewish Celebration

This menu combines two traditional Jewish dishes from two different holidays—potato pancakes served at Hanukkah, and haroset, a sweet fruit dish served at the Seder, or Passover. Of course, they would not be served at the same meal, traditionally, but you can introduce them to children with a little background about Jewish holidays. The unusual twist to the potato pancakes is that already-prepared frozen hash browns are used instead of raw potatoes as a delicious but quick way to make this favorite dish.

Potato Pancakes

INGREDIENTS:

1 ½ CUPS HASH BROWNS
1 TABLESPOON CHOPPED ONION
1 EGG, BEATEN
1 TABLESPOON BREAD CRUMBS
SALT and PEPPER to TASTE
COOKING OIL

METHOD:

POTATO PANCAKES

1. SLIGHTLY THAW the FROZEN, SHREDDED HASH BROWNS by LETTING THEM SIT OUT of the FREEZER. MIX THEM with the ONION, BEATEN EGG, BREAD CRUMBS, SALT and PEPPER.
2. HEAT OIL in FRYING PAN, and DROP HEAPING SPOONFULS of the POTATO MIXTURE in OIL. FRY on ONE SIDE a FEW MINUTES, GENTLY TURN OVER, and FRY on the OTHER SIDE.
3. SERVE with SOUR CREAM and APPLESAUCE CONDIMENTS.

Haroset

INGREDIENTS:
3 chopped apples
1 cup chopped nuts
⅓ cup grape juice
½ teaspoon cinnamon
1 tablespoon honey
Bowls of the sour cream and
    applesauce for the table

METHOD:

HAROSET

1. Chop apples and add to the chopped nuts.
2. Stir in other ingredients.
3. Serve as a side dish.

Appendix

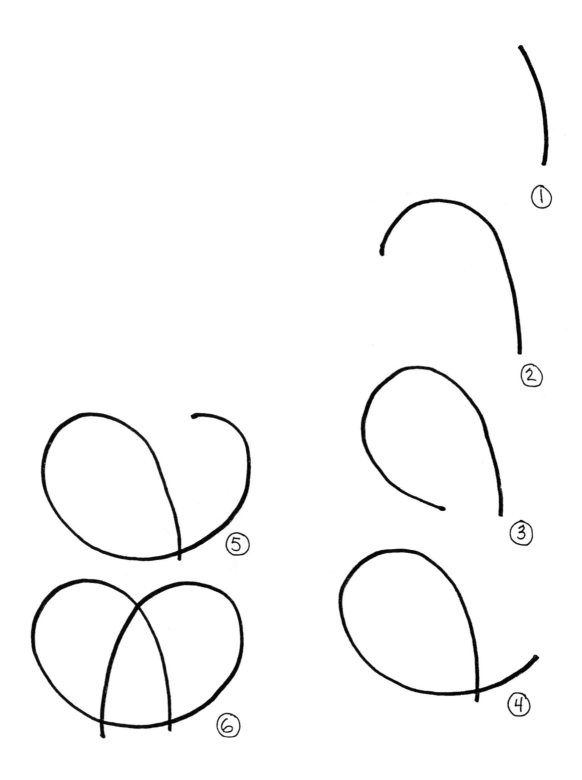

Resource Bibliography

Better Homes and Gardens. *Healthy Foods for Hungry Kids.* Better Homes and Gardens, 1987.

Good-for-you ingredients in tasty food. Lots of kid preparation possible.

Better Homes and Gardens. *Kid's Lunches.* Better Homes and Gardens, 1986.

Appealing color photographs inspire very different lunches such as Robot Rounds and Top-of-the-6th Chicken. Includes clear directions, and many dishes are designed for microwave preparation.

Better Homes and Gardens. *Microwave Cooking for Kids.* Better Homes and Gardens, 1984.

Simple, microwave instructions have kid appeal and minimal cleanup.

Better Homes and Gardens. *Step by Step Kid's Cookbook.* Better Homes and Gardens, 1984.

This book includes easy-to-make dishes from snacks to a full meal. Directions indicate which steps need adult help.

Blain, Diane. *The Boxcar Children Cookbook.* Illustrated by L. Kate Deal and Eileen Mueller Neill. Albert Whitman, 1991.

Recipes inspired by foods mentioned in the popular series about the Boxcar Children include Snowstorm Spaghetti and Meat Sauce, Hobo Stew, and Lighthouse Brownies. Quotes from the books preface each recipe.

Cox, Beverly, and Martin Jacobs. *Spirit of the Harvest.* Stewart, Tabori & Chang, 1991.

This book of Native-American food is organized by geographic region. Each section contains specific information on growing and preparation of various food's use in the celebration and life of the native Americans of that region, and recipes. The book contains maps and photographs, and provides good background for leaders to develop multicultural units around the topic of food.

Coyle, Rena. *My First Cookbook.* Illustrated by Jerry Joyner. Workman, 1985.

This step-by-step illustrated cookbook provides 50 recipes for breakfast, lunch, dinner, holidays, and special occasions. Safety tips and fun food facts are included.

Dineen, Jacqueline. *Chocolate.* Carolrhoda, 1990.

This introductory book on chocolate tells where it comes from and how it is processed and made into cocoa powder and chocolate bars. Includes a history and recipes. It is part of a Food We Eat series that includes books on apples, beans and peas, bread, butter, cheese, citrus fruits, eggs, rice, meat, milk, pasta, potatoes, sugar, and vegetables.

Drake, Christin Fjeld. *The Sleepy Baker. A Collection of Stories and Recipes for Children.* Illustrated by Alexandra Eldridge. Northland Publishing, 1993.

Twelve original stories based on Norwegian folk tales, each with a recipe.

Drew, Helen. *My First Baking Book.* Knopf, 1991.

Clear step-by-step recipes, with photographs in full color, describe sweet baked goods such as cookies, shortbread, and cupcakes.

Greene, Karen. *Once Upon a Recipe.* New Hope, 1987.

This book includes all kinds of literature-related recipes, from "Over the Rainbow Milk" to "Velveteen Rabbit Soup."

Irving, Jan, and Robin Currie. *Mudluscious: Stories and Activities Featuring Food for Preschool Children.* Libraries Unlimited, 1986.

This popular resource book combines stories, rhymes, crafts, recipes, and whole language activities on the topic of food.

Kenda, Margaret, and Phyllis S. Williams. *Cooking Wizardry for Kids.* Barrons, 1990.

This packaged deal includes a chef hat, apron, and a 312-page cookbook filled with recipes and food experiments.

Lansky, Vicki. *Microwave Cooking for Kids.* Scholastic, 1991.

An elementary guide for beginning cooks using the safe and convenient microwave. Ingredient needs are given in cup and spoon, and metric measure.

Machotka, Hana. *Pasta Factory.* Houghton Mifflin, 1992.

Photographs and informational text give the fascinating account of a class taking a trip through the Tutta Pasta Factory in New Jersey. Names for a wide variety of pasta shapes are explained, and the processing of pasta is described in detail.

Moore, Eva. *The Great Banana Cookbook for Boys and Girls.* Illustrated by Susan Russo. Clarion, 1983.

Eleven simple recipes for banana treats include salads, breads and muffins, and cookies. With banana facts.

Nottridge, Rhoda. *Vitamins.* Carolrhoda, 1992.

Facts about vitamins as well as science experiments, recipes, nutritional background and meal planning are included in this book, part of the "Food Facts" series. Other topics in the series are additives, fats, fiber, proteins, and sugars.

Roop, Peter, and Connie Roop. *Out to Lunch!* Illustrated by Joan Hanson. Lerner, 1984.

These jokes about food will inspire kids to write their own.

Scobey, Joan. *The Fannie Farmer Junior Cookbook.* Illustrated by Patience Brewster. Little, Brown, 1993.

This new edition offers a variety of recipes with simple kitchen tips and meal plans.

Shapiro, Rebecca. *Wide World Cookbook.* Little, Brown, 1962.

Recipes from over 50 countries represent a wide variety of foods, each given an introduction about the food and eating customs in the individual countries.

Stallworth, Lyn. *Wond'rous Fare.* Illustrated by Jim Bennett, Dennis Dittrick, John Hayes, and Jim Robinson. A Calico Book, Contemporary Books, 1988.

Inspired by food mentioned in favorite children's books, the author has imaginatively given recipes for food that may even be mentioned in the books. Recipes include Jack's Beanstalk Salad, King of Tarts Ham Sandwich, and Henny Penny's Pancakes.

Stewart, Janet M., ed. *Kid's Party Cookbook.* Hayes Publishing, 1988.

Part of the I Can Do This series, this title has two to four recipes under each of a dozen topics. For example, "Party Pizzas" has two recipes, one for an English muffin pizza and one for a fruit pizza. The brightly colored pictures and lists of ingredients make it an appealing and useful cookbook for kids.

Supraner, Robyn. *Quick and Easy Cookbook.* Illustrated by Renzo Barto. Troll Associates, 1981.

Over 20 recipes with pictures and step-by-step instructions. Also includes a listing of utensils needed for each recipe.

Waters, Alice. *Fanny at Chez Panisse.* Illustrated by Ann Arnold. HarperCollins, 1992.

Stories and recipes tell about seven-year-old Fanny's adventures in her mother's restaurant in Berkley, California.

Wilkes, Angela. *My First Cook Book.* Knopf, 1989.

Large page format, big, bright photographs, and step-by-step instructions in words and pictures explain procedures for making such treats as cookies, ice cream sundaes, speedy pizzas, and mini quiches.

Wilkes, Angela. *My First Party Book.* Knopf, 1991.

Besides recipes for funny-face dips and birthday cakes, this book includes ideas for invitations and favors.

Williamson, Sarah, and Zachary Williamson. *Kids Cook!* Illustrated by Loretta Trezzo-Braren. Williamson Publishing, 1992.

Besides recipes for sandwiches, snacks, and desserts, there are step-by-step instructions, notes about processes, safety alerts, and nutrition notes.

Winston, Mary, ed. *American Heart Association Kids' Cookbook.* Random House, 1993.

Good and good-for-you snacks and meals for health-conscious kids and teachers.

Wolfe, Robert, and Diane Wolfe. *Holiday Cooking Around the World.* Lerner, 1988.

This easy ethnic cookbook introduces the role of food in holiday celebrations around the world. The recipes are from 15 different countries and would be enjoyed most during the winter holiday season. Other titles in this series teach about cooking in Africa, Israel, Lebanon, Mexico, Thailand, and Vietnam.

Young, Caroline. *The Usborne Round the World Cookbook.* Illustrated by Nadine Wickenden. Usborne, 1993.

Some unusually delicious recipes from 21 places, and Jewish fare, are attractively illustrated. Food facts and customs, in addition to geographical notes, make the cookbook useful for teachers and librarians planning multicultural units and programs.

Author-Title Index

About the Authors

Jan Irving (on the left) has been a teacher, a children's librarian, and a visiting professor of children's library services at the University of Iowa's School of Library Science. She was a 1984 recipient of the Putnam Publishing Award, sponsored by the Association for Library Service to Children of the American Library Association. Along with the six books (*Mudluscious, Glad Rags, Full Speed Ahead, Raising the Roof, From the Heart,* and *Straw Into Gold*) with Robin Currie, Jan has authored *Fanfares: Programs for Classrooms and Libraries* for Libraries Unlimited, and coordinated the state summer library programs for the State Library of Iowa. Jan currently lives in St. Paul, Minnesota with her husband.

Robin Currie (on the right) has been active in state-wide children's library services, coordinating the development of summer programs in Iowa and Illinois. In addition to the six books (*Mudluscious, Glad Rags, Full Speed Ahead, Raising the Roof, From the Heart,* and *Straw Into Gold*) with Jan Irving, Robin has written two books for the Iowa State Library: *Rainbows and Ice Cream: Storytimes About Things Kids Like,* and *Double Rainbows: More Storytimes About Things Kids Like*. Robin lives in the Chicago suburbs and manages the children's book department at Anderson's Bookshop in Elmhurst. She is currently a graduate student at the Lutheran School of Theology at Chicago studying for the ordained ministry.